FRONT PAGE 97
A YEAR OF CHANGE

Tom Brden
197.
D.c.

£7.99

This pictorial account of 1997 shows an amazing year of change and tragedy as seen through some of the Front Pages of Scotland's two leading newspapers

ISBN 1 901603 05 9

193/197 Bath Street, Glasgow, G2 4HU
Telephone: 0141 226 2200. Fax: 0141 248 1099

Published by First Press Publishing Limited
193-197 Bath Street, Glasgow G2 4HU
© Daily Record and Sunday Mail

ACKNOWLEDGEMENTS

The Daily Record and Sunday Mail
would like to thank
their loyal readers and staff
for their continuing contributions
to the success of
Scotland's champion newspapers

You can't beat the Record

The Sunday Mail – the Heart of Scotland

1997
A Year of Change

"IT was the best of times, it was the worst of times . . . it was the season of Light, it was the season of Darkness, it was the spring of hope, it was the winter of despair . . ."

The famous first sentence of Charles Dickens' novel, A Tale of Two Cities, certainly applied to 1997.

It was always going to be a historic year. Change was in the air when it opened.

The national mood was one of waiting for it to happen.

The people knew that, in the General Election, they would soon have a chance to decide on a new future for Britain. When the time came, they seized that chance.

A decayed and discredited order was replaced by one of promise and optimism.

Nowhere more so than in Scotland, where the people created their own "new dawn".

What no-one could know was the shadow that would be cast by a shockingly sudden and unnecessary tragedy – and how the death of one young woman would move millions.

In life, Princess Diana was an international icon of glamour. In death, she became a phenomenon and the focus for a nation's sense of loss.

The real-life wretchedness of Diana's fairy-tale marriage was receding into memory and – although there were lapses into soap opera Royalty – she was finding a new role as a campaigner for compassionate causes.

As mother of the future King, her place in the public eye was assured. Her popularity grew with every caring image, while support for the Monarchy itself and for individual members of the Royal Family was on the wane.

New Prime Minister Tony Blair summed up her status when he said she was "The People's Princess".

The suddenness and violence of Diana's death, at the age of 36, in a horrific and needless car crash, stunned the world.

The circumstances – as she sat in the rear of a limousine beside her new lover Dodi Fayed, with a drunk driver at the wheel trying to escape from the pursuit of the ever-present paparazzi – made the loss even more pointless.

The effect of her death was exceptional. It created an emotional shock wave that numbed the nation, then unleashed a torrent of emotion that swept the country.

It brought public life in Britain to a halt and united the people in a way no other event could have done.

The traditional British reserve collapsed in a show of communal grief.

The flood of messages, the avalanche of flowers that carpeted the pavements around the palaces, the queues of mourners, the uncanny silence that descended on Britain on the day of her funeral, all testified that she had indeed become what she had wanted to be – "a queen of people's hearts".

Diana's legacy remains to be seen. Changes in the style of the British Monarchy have been promised.

They were essential if it was to survive into the 21st century. Diana's death, and the public reaction to it, made the modernising and humanising of the Monarchy inevitable.

Prime Minister Blair urged Britain to become a more caring nation in memory of Diana.

He was echoing his own words, spoken on the steps of 10 Downing Street on the day he took power, when he had called for "one Britain, one nation, in which our ambition for ourselves is matched by our sense of compassion and decency and duty towards other people".

Blair became Prime Minister because the people had decided it was time for a change – and that was what he offered. Just as he had renewed the Labour Party, he promised to renew and rejuvenate Britain.

After 18 years of Tory government, Britain had become increasingly divided between haves and have-nots, prosperous and poor, workers and workless, housed and homeless, those who could pay for care and those who had to queue for care.

The Tories, with the arrogance of unbroken power, had become squabbling, self-serving and sleaze-ridden.

The result, at the General Election, was a political earthquake. Labour's victory was so total that it caused a seismic shift in Britain's political landscape and swept the Conservatives out of Scotland, Wales and the English cities.

For Scotland, it meant an opportunity to make history, assert Scottish nationhood and right an old wrong – all in one.

The long-held dream of a Scottish Parliament could become a reality IF the Scots wanted it enough. After decades of disappointment, years of frustration under minority Tory Ministers in Edinburgh and the letdown of the 1979 referendum, the new Labour Government was committed to delivering devolution.

The final hurdle was the referendum, designed to demonstrate that home rule really was – in the oft-quoted words of the late John Smith – "the settled will of the Scottish people".

There was always a doubt that Scots would funk it or wouldn't care enough so that, once again, Scotland would wake up with a national hangover and nothing to show for it.

For once, the Scottish talent for self-destruction was replaced by a bold self-belief. There was no slip-up, no betrayal, no letdown. The Scottish Parliament was triumphantly confirmed by a three-to-one vote on September 11.

Because, of all the things that were different after the Year of Change, the most significant was the nation's mood. The people had found a new confidence and taken control of their own destiny.

In Scotland, it wasn't Braveheart bravado but a quiet, controlled determination that Scots could – and should – run their own lives.

1997 was a year to remember. It had its moment of overwhelming sadness. But, above all, it was the end of a dark age – and a new beginning.

Lament for a Dead Princess

THROUGHOUT the year, the twin strands of Princess Diana's life – public and private – interwove and criss-crossed.

There was Diana's personal mission of mercy as she created the role she had claimed for herself – Queen of Hearts.

In January came the image that will be remembered, along with dazzling designer-dressed Diana.

This was the Princess in a flak jacket on the battlefield, campaigning for a world-wide ban on anti-personnel land mines.

And, of course, the compassionate Diana comforting a 13-year-old girl who had lost a leg, and a soldier waiting to be fitted with two artificial legs. "Horrific," she told reporters. "This puts everything into perspective."

Enraged Tory MPs and peers attacked her as "a loose cannon", words they came to regret.

In reply, the princess gave a hint of her motivation: "I have seen some horrifying things over the years but I've learned to cope with it because each person is an individual – each person needs a bit of love . . ."

The statement rang with echoes of her troubled childhood and her disastrous marriage. It was to be remembered seven months later.

Diana's life seemed to be a search for love, a search for a role in life. She gave what no other royal gave – genuine warmth, often with an impulsive touch or a hug.

She gave love but rarely got what she really wanted – love in return. Except from her sons, from others who shared her vulnerability or the less fortunate.

There were other caring images. Diana meeting her hero, Nelson Mandela, and offering to help fight the AIDS epidemic raging through South Africa: "If I can help in any way, I'm available."

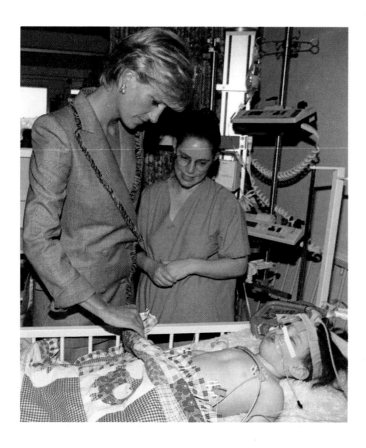

Diana holding a toddler's hand as she recovered on a life-support machine in a children's intensive care unit.

Diana at an AIDS hospice.

Diana talking to girl victims of eating disorders and admitting she was still haunted by bulimia: "I could go back to it, but it's not an option."

Diana in traditional Pakistani costume visiting Imran Khan's cancer hospital.

Diana selling her designer gowns for AIDS. Shrewdly, she chose New York for the auction and the royalty-mad Americans paid an astonishing £2 million for her cast-offs.

Diana in black, comforting a weeping Elton John in Milan Cathedral at the funeral of the murdered Italian designer Gianni Versace.

Significantly, the Princess's love-hate relationship with the media surfaced in April when she begged for protection from photographers.

Palace aides and police criticised her for becoming involved in a scuffle with a paparazzo who ambushed her from behind a tree as she left her London gym.

No-one could have known it, but her reply was a portent of grim events to come: "The Princess hopes that the recently-passed Protection from Harassment Act will give greater protection to people such as herself, who are the victims of this kind of distressing intrusion into their private lives."

Of course, it was the Princess's private life that was the subject of fascination.

There was a flurry when she slipped away from her official round in Pakistan to pay a secret visit to the family of heart surgeon Hasnat Khan, with whom she had been linked in London.

With due dignity, his father commented: "If my son and the princess asked me for my permission to marry, I would consider it."

Just two months later, in July, the Princess's love-life took a different – and fateful – turn.

The seeds of tragedy were sown on a care-free holiday in the Mediterranean sun. At the time, Diana's cruise with her sons William and Harry aboard Harrods tycoon Mohammed Al Fayed's yacht was interesting only because of her host.

The Daily Record commented: "Al Fayed's seedy role in the cash-for-questions affair makes him a far-from-suit-able holiday host.

"Not for the first time, when it comes to matters of judgment, Di's all at sea."

Also aboard were Al Fayed's family, including his 41-year-old son Dodi.

At the time, the possibility of a relationship with the dashing Dodi was overlooked. After all, everything was against him. He was an Egyptian Muslim, known as a playboy film producer, who seemed to have his pick of Hollywood-style beauties, including the dishy Daryl Hannah and a stunning model who later claimed he had promised to marry her.

He was hardly a suitable partner for the mother of the future King, was he . . . ?

Yet there were other clues to the new romance, which the royal watchers failed to pick up. In an impromptu talk with journalists as they bobbed on the water, Di seemed to be preparing the ground for a new departure.

"My boys are urging me continually to leave the country," she told them. "Maybe that's what I should do."

Back in Britain, Charles was courting unwanted publicity by throwing a 50th birthday party for his lover Camilla Parker Bowles and giving her a £100,000 diamond bracelet.

On August 7, it was front-page news: "Di's New Man – The Look of Love". She had enjoyed a secret six days aboard the yacht off Corsica before they were spotted by the paparazzi.

Next day, on the eve of her departure for Bosnia, Diana openly turned up on the doorstep of Dodi's London home. Dinner for two was delivered on silver platters.

What more could the gossip writers ask for?

Sadly, it was all might-have-been.
In the early hours of Sunday, August 31, the shattering news emerged and we woke to the Sunday Mail's stark front page:

Even in the boldest of headline type, the reaction was that it couldn't be true. The nation, the world, caught its breath in disbelief and shock.

Quite simply, there is no other person in the world whose death would have stunned so many, caused such a universal sense of loss and hurt, sent such a ripple of deep regret around the globe.

The media scrambled to answer the questions the world was asking.

Radio and TV scrapped their schedules and went over to a rolling news menu of the facts, as they filtered in, and sorrowful comment.

But it is always the case that with news of such magnitude, only newspapers can provide the width and depth of coverage to match the event. Let's face it, many people could not accept that the tragedy had actually taken place until they read, re-read and absorbed the detailed accounts.

The Sunday Mail and Daily Record launched a unique operation. Round-the-clock special editions rolled off the presses as staff worked throughout the night and continued through the day.

And it is striking how that instant reportage and analysis stands the test of hindsight.

From Saturday night into Sunday afternoon, the Sunday Mail's front page changed six times, culminating in a remembrance edition that remains a souvenir of that sombre Sunday.

The Mail gave the first accounts after the Mercedes smashed into the concrete pillar in a Paris underpass, killing Diana, Dodi Fayed and driver Henri Paul and seriously injuring British bodyguard.

And the Mail also began the assessment of the life and death of "one of the most famous women of the 20th Century . . . certainly the most photographed . . ."

The Sunday Mail spoke of a nation plunged into a deep pit of sorrow: "She used who she was to help those less fortunate than herself. Diana had a fragility about her they recognised in themselves.

"There are many who cannot abide the Monarchy and who would like to see the archaic system of royalty swept away.

"There are those who regarded Diana as nothing more than a celebrity, a British answer to the film stars America has in abundance.

"Yet today Diana is dead and the very idea seems an insult to all logic and sense.

"For ultimately, Diana was more than just Diana, more than just a princess.

"Diana was – and is – irreplaceable."

The Daily Record took over with unprecedented Sunday afternoon editions, rolling into Monday. It kept pace as the tragedy unfolded.

And it was quick to pick up on the most remarkable aspect of the Diana tragedy – the sudden and immediate surge of public emotion.

That sense of loss, coupled with Diana's status as an icon of glamour and personal sadness, evoked a spontaneous response which became a phenomenon.

Strangely, Diana's lasting legacy will be the void that she left. More than anything, the remarkable response to her death seemed a symptom of the nation's spiritual emptiness.

Something was missing from people's lives, something that patriotism, heroes, saints living or dead, did not meet.

The Record View reflected that feeling: "An ordinary member of the public, one of Princess Diana's legion of admirers, delivered this perfect epitaph on the Queen of Hearts: 'A light has gone out.'

"Now she will become a legend.

"People will remember the Sunday they woke to the news.

"Her sudden, needless and violent death will ensure her memory is preserved at the height of her beauty and womanhood.

"And she will forever be the sad symbol of the misused and misunderstood woman."

The Record also led the clamour for the Princess to be buried with full State honours. It was obvious that the Establishment (whom Diana had labelled 'the enemy') wanted a low-key funeral, but they quickly had to bow to the public insistence on a proper farewell for the People's Princess.

Again, the Sunday Mail and Daily Record produced impressive souvenir editions of an extraordinary day, when Britain fell uncannily silent.

Two voices, however, will be remembered from that day. Elton John singing the lyric that equated Diana with another popular icon: "You lived your life like a candle in the wind. Your candle's burned out long before your legend ever will . . ."

And the voice of Diana's brother, Earl Spencer – "the representative of a family in grief in a country in mourning before a world in shock" – in a bitter blast at the media. Also, in implied indictment of the Royal Family, pledging that her "blood family" would see that the Princes William and Harry were brought up in her way – "so that their souls are not simply immersed by duty and tradition but can sing openly as you planned."

His withering words brought another instant response, the sound of applause that started in the street outside, burst through the open doors, echoed around the abbey and throughout the nation.

Said the Record: "It must have sounded like the thunder of an approaching storm for the Queen and her family."

There were lessons to be learned all round – by the media, by the Palace and by the public.

True, Diana's image sold billions of copies of newspapers and magazines. The media fed a voracious public appetite. She had been a skilled manipulator of the media, when it suited her purpose.

That she appeared to have been literally hounded to death by the paparazzi, who knew an off-guard, revealing shot could earn them huge amounts of money, triggered understandable demands to curb such harassment.

Britain's national newspaper editors agreed a new code on the use of such photographs and pledged protection for privacy, particularly of the young princes.

For the House of Windsor, the year had started badly and ended disastrously. In January, a poll for an ITV programme, Monarchy –
The Nation Decides, showed the depth of dissatisfaction.

UK-wide, 66 per cent were in favour of the Monarchy, with 34 per cent against. In Scotland, however, 56 per cent said 'No' to the continuation of the Monarchy – and it is a matter of speculation what these figures might have been if the poll had been taken at the other end of the year.

With respect for royalty on the wane and fast disappearing in Scotland, Diana's death – following what many saw as callous treatment of a vulnerable young woman –

caused a crisis of confidence, verging on hostility.

On the eve of the funeral, in the face of the overpowering wave of pro-Diana emotion, the Queen was compelled to address the nation "from my heart".

Her key message was the acknowledgement: "I, for one, believe that there are lessons to be drawn from her life and from the extraordinary and moving reaction to her death."

The queen's personal tribute to Diana – "an exceptional and gifted human being" as princess and mother – was seen as an attempt to make amends and signal acceptance of her subjects' need for a warmer, kindlier approach.

In fact, a Diana-style Monarchy!

Tony's Triumph
A Major Disaster

THE 1997 General Election was an inevitable victory – which turned into an unbelievable landslide.

It had its weird and wonderful moments. The Tories trotted out an actor in a chicken costume to taunt Tony Blair on the campaign trail. A fox was sent after the chicken.

The Scottish Nationalists unleashed three Scots terriers to take on the bulldog which featured in a Labour TV broadcast.

It was all light relief from this century's longest election. The Tory tactic of a six-week campaign was meant to give them time to wear down Labour's lead and allow Labour time to make mistakes. Neither happened.

At the start, polls showed Labour with a lead of between 15 and 25 per cent. One even showed Scotland's safest Tory seat, the sleaze-hit Eastwood, falling to Labour.

Few believed the figures. It was inconceivable that supporters would desert the Conservative cause in such numbers. Until the final count, John Major insisted that the polls were "rubbish".

In fact, on polling day, the voters gave Labour a 14 per cent lead and Tony Blair became Prime Minister with a landslide majority of 179. And Scotland became a Tory-free zone, as even Eastwood fell to Labour.

The Tories recorded their lowest share of the vote in their party's history, as the parties reversed what had become their traditional roles. It was the Tories who were divided, ill-disciplined and lacking leadership.

Labour were well-drilled and united behind a strong and single-minded leader. At their headquarters in Millbank Tower, London, they had the most formidable election machine, slick and hi-tech, with relentless "spin-doctoring", "rapid rebuttal" and rigid adherence to "staying on message".

Prime Minister John Major had a miserable election, unable to damp down the dissent in his own ranks and repeatedly betrayed by his back-benchers.

In desperation, he scrapped Conservative Central Office strategy and resorted to a basic appeal, relying on his own niceness and personal integrity.

However, the Honest John approach, which had saved the Tory bacon in 1992, backfired badly in 1997.

The voters took the message that John might be honest, but his party wasn't.

The final nail in the Conservative coffin was one word: SLEAZE.

After 18 years of power, they were already perceived as tired and out-of-touch. They had forfeited their reputation as the business-like party that could handle the economy. Throughout their last Parliament and during the election campaign, they squabbled among themselves over Europe and a range of other issues, to the point where their leader had to submit to a humiliating "back me or sack me" ploy. And, although he won the leadership vote, John Major was never the man Margaret Thatcher was!

Scotland had a special score to settle. The legacy of the Thatcher years was a reputation for arrogance and insensitivity to Scotland's needs. Resentment grew that Scots returned Labour majorities, yet were governed by a tiny Tory minority.

Successive Conservative Secretaries of State for Scotland were seen as little more than colonial governors – and the last, the pugnacious political street-fighter Michael Forsyth, was unpopular even with a sizeable section of his own party.

And added to all that was sleaze . . .

Sex scandals had already tarnished the Tory image, but a string of financial misdemeanours proved more damaging. They culminated in the "cash for questions" affair, with allegations of Tory MPs pocketing brown envelopes stuffed with banknotes.

In Eastwood, the Tory outpost to the south of Glasgow, troubled MP Allan Stewart – a man liked and respected even by his political opponents – quit after stories about his private life. It was a personal tragedy but it became worse for his party.

Scottish Tory chairman Sir Michael Hirst was touted for the seat but had to withdraw, admitting to "past indiscretions" amid reports of a gay affair. Hirst claimed he was a victim of smear tactics and it emerged that the smears came from within the chaotic Conservative Party.

As a result, the Tories were written off in Scotland before they even began campaigning. When their separate manifesto for Scotland was launched, it was immediately dubbed "Forsyth's Farewell".

The election campaign had been running for months before the "off" was officially signalled. In February, the future Chancellor Gordon Brown made a pre-emptive strike by promising there would be no income tax increases in the first five years of a Labour Government.

In March, Tony Blair came to Inverness to address the Scottish Labour Conference, seen as New Labour in the last stronghold of "old" Labour. He won them over with a surprisingly emotional off-the-cuff appeal, telling them traditional Labour values still held and urging them: "Have a little faith."

The Labour leader was given a rough ride over devolution on his campaign visits to Scotland, with suggestions that he was lukewarm on the Scottish Parliament and wanted to curb its tax-varying power. He turned the tables by challenging Scotland: "Back me and I WILL deliver a Scottish Parliament – if YOU want it."

Blair's aim was to turn attention from the devolution debate to the issues important to community-conscious Scotland – education, health, unemployment, particularly jobs for young Scots, and creating a safe and decent society. Tackling these AND giving Scots control over their own affairs proved a winning formula.

Throughout, a cautious Blair warned his followers not to take the result for granted. On the eve of polling day, he predicted he would have a majority of 30 seats – and ended up with nearly six times that figure.

On May 2, he entered No. 10 declaring to the crowd outside and the wider world: "For 18 long years, my party has been in opposition. It could only say, it could not do.

"Today, enough of talking – it is time now to do."

He immediately started "doing", forming a Cabinet with a strong Scottish element, and the flurry of new policies and initiatives in the next months showed how impatient he had been for power.

The Tories began picking among the debris of defeat for their way forward. In place of the defeated John Major, they elected the boyish William Hague, who promised "A Fresh Start".

But it was obvious the nation had also decided on a fresh start – without the Conservatives.

Scotland's New Dawn

THE election result had a direct effect in Scotland. The promised referendum on home rule for Scots was set for September 11.

New Scottish Secretary Donald Dewar produced a widely-acclaimed devolution White Paper – in effect, the blueprint for the new Scottish Parliament and its powers – which became an instant best-seller.

Three of the parties who had been fierce opponents in the General Election – Labour, Liberal Democrat and the SNP – united to persuade the Scottish people to vote Yes-Yes in the two-question referendum on the Parliament and its tax-varying power.

The Conservatives continued their implacable opposition to the scheme, resorting to scare tactics about the break-up of the United Kingdom.

Their negative No-No campaign only confirmed why Scots had rejected them and proved they had learned nothing from their election disaster.

For the second time in four-and-a-half months, the voters confounded even the wildest expectations. Although the referendum campaign was interrupted by the period of national mourning for Princess Diana, the result was emphatic.

A startling 74 per cent supported the establishment of the Scottish Parliament and an even more surprising 63 per cent voted to give it tax-varying powers.

A relieved Prime Minister Blair – his much-criticised referendum stratagem overwhelmingly vindicated – was cheered by a jubilant crowd in Edinburgh's historic Parliament Square.

"Well done!" he told them. "This is a good day for Scotland and a good day for the United Kingdom."

As they woke up to their "new dawn", celebrating Scots agreed.

Month by Month

WHAT makes a Page One story? Important, bizarre, controversial, glamorous, sensational, outrageous, tragic, exclusive . . .

It can be all of these things, but it has to have the indefinable factor that grabs and holds the reader's attention and sells newspapers.

Month by month, the front pages show who and what made the news . . .

December

Two British nurses in Saudi Arabia – Lucille McLauchlan from Dundee, and Deborah Parry from Hampshire – were charged with the murder of Australian colleague Yvonne Gilford.

Fears that they would receive harsh justice under Islamic law proved justified. Months later, Parry was sentenced to beheading and Lucy McLauchlan to jail and 500 lashes as an accessory.

In the months that followed, there were international protests against the inhumane sentences and pleas for mercy. But it took the payment of "blood money" to the victim's brother in Australia before there was a possibility that the sentences would be commuted.

January

The year began badly with the "Hogmanay from Hell" – or so it seemed to many.

Temperatures plunged as low as minus 10 as hundreds of thousands of revellers took to the streets and travellers trying to get home to their families were hit by snowbound roads and rail strike chaos.

After the world's biggest Hogmanay party in Edinburgh's Princes Street, 300 people ended up in hospital and the crush of 350,000 revellers was blamed. The truth was that most had drunk themselves into oblivion.

On the football front, Kenny Dalglish took over as manager of Newcastle United on a £1 million-a-year contract. The former Celtic, Liverpool and Scotland star was already a millionaire – not bad for a former apprentice joiner.

February

There were tears of joy as the Bridgewater Three left jail after 19 years. Vincent and Michael Hickey and Jim Robertson walked free after a High Court declared police had faked the evidence that condemned them for the murder of a newspaper boy. But the fourth, Pat Molloy, didn't live to see his name cleared – he died in prison in 1981.

The Daily Record launched its campaign to save children from the perverts who prey on them. A shocking dossier of evidence showed how the law, government and the system were all failing to protect Scotland's youngsters. The Record's Charter for Children – most of which was later enacted by the new Labour administration at the Scottish Office – was supported by a flood of heart-rending calls from victims of child abuse.

March

The Daily Record and the Sunday Mail marked the poignant first anniversary of the tragedy Scotland will never forget, the massacre of the innocents in Dunblane Primary School.

The Record distributed a million candles and, on the evening of the anniversary, the lights shone out from windows throughout the land and all round the world.

The Sunday Mail's book, written with the full co-operation of the parents and people of Dunblane, told the harrowing story of the tragedy, lest anyone forget . . .

By the end of the year, Dunblane: Our Year of Tears had raised £50,000, which was presented to Princess Anne for the Save the Children Fund.

April

The Grand National, the world's most famous steeplechase, was cancelled because of an IRA bomb scare.

The interference with one of the blue riband events in the British sporting calendar caused equal measures of disappointment and defiance.

The race was run on the Monday, amid unprecedented security. Prime Minister John Major turned up to show his solidarity with the punters, who declared they would not give in to the terrorists.

When it finally took place, the '97 National proved to be a thriller. It was won by Lord Gyllene, ridden by Tony Dobbin, who led the rest of the field from start to finish.

The miners of Monktonhall, who had sunk their savings into saving their pit, were thrown on the slag heap. The 300 were sacked without warning as the pit was declared unviable leaving Scotland's once-proud coal industry with only one deep mine.

May

Glasgow Govan MP Mohammed Sarwar, who had only won the seat on May 1 after a bitter selection battle, was accused of bribing a General Election rival.

Photographs showed him handing over £5,000 in a plastic bag to his former rival. Sarwar insisted it was a loan, not a bribe, but the Labour Party suspended him and the police launched an investigation.

The Spice Girls showed what "Girl Power" was all about by patting Prince Charles on the bottom and leaving lipstick smackers on his face. Charles didn't seem to know whether to be amused or embarrassed.

Rangers achieved a record-equalling, nine-in-a-row league championships. It was all the sweeter because the feat finally put them on a par with Old Firm rivals Celtic's run in the Sixties and Seventies.

June

Oasis star Noel Gallagher married his long-term girlfriend at the Little Church of the West in Las Vegas, where Elvis Presley married Priscilla. Just to show there was still some life left in old rockers, it was revealed that Mick Jagger was to become a father at 54.

To many people's surprise, including his own party's, William Hague was elected Tory leader at the age of 36.

Prime Minister Tony Blair began the process that was to lead to the Northern Ireland peace talks, saying: "If we don't move this forward now, then I really fear for the future."

The sun finally set on the British Empire as China took back Hong Kong. The Black Watch were among the last troops to march out, and the Union Flag was folded and carried aboard the Britannia by two Scots sailors.

July

In a year heavy with bereavement, two Hollywood legends – tough guy Robert Mitchum and the laconic James Stewart – died within hours of each other.

Fashion guru Gianni Versace was shot dead at point-blank range at the gates of his Miami mansion. His gay killer, Andrew Cunahan, was later found to have committed suicide. At the exceptionally well-dressed funeral in Italy, Princess Diana comforted a weeping Elton John.

Paisley South MP Gordon McMaster, who had been battling against illness, committed suicide in his garage.

The note he left – saying he had been driven to his death by a smear campaign – caused political turmoil which lasted for months.

The Labour Party was forced to hold another probe into allegations of sleaze and vicious in-fighting among MPs.

Neighbouring MP Tommy Graham (West Renfrewshire) was suspended under investigation for bringing the Labour Party into disrepute.

Celtic finally landed a manager, Dutchman Wim Jansen, who was to be paid £1.5 million on a three-year contract to restore the Glasgow club to its former glory – and put them back on a par with Rangers.

August

Foreign Secretary Robin Cook left his wife for his secretary Gaynor Regan, admitting : "The responsibility is entirely mine." Whereas in the previous government it might have been a resignation matter, Prime Minister Blair signalled his confidence in his Cabinet colleague.

"Big Mags" Heaney, the mother of the notorious "family from hell" was forced to leave her home in Stirling's Raploch district by a 400-strong doorstep demonstration. Hundreds more had signed a petition to Stirling Council, demanding her eviction. Ironically, "Big Mags" had been the leader of a vigilante campaign to drive sex offenders from their homes in the area.

September

Six passengers were killed and 160 injured when an express train crashed into freight wagons in London. The disaster raised questions about rail safety under the piecemeal privatisation of the rail system.

Nine Glasgow councillors, including Lord Provost Pat Lally, were suspended as the Labour Party began yet another sleaze investigation into the "votes for trips" affair. The Lord Provost protested: "This is condemnation without trial – I want justice."

Europe's golfers won the Ryder Cup against the US in Spain. The victory was clinched by Scot Colin Montgomerie.

October

The risks taken by Scotland's fishermen were brought home yet again when four died as the Peterhead trawler Sapphire was sunk by a freak wave "as quickly as a handclap".

Prime Minister Blair received a rude reminder that peace would not come easy in Northern Ireland. After shaking the hand of Sinn Fein's Gerry Adams, he ran a gauntlet of Loyalist hate and was taunted with rubber gloves.

The Record's campaign to curb child abusers scored another success when it was announced that offenders would be subjected to DNA finger-printing. Child molesters would also face double sentences – a jail term followed by a period of strict probation, during which they must stay away from schools, playparks and other locations.

Scotland qualified for the World Cup football finals in France in 1998 with a 2-0 victory over Latvia.

November

In a US trial that became compulsive TV on both sides of the Atlantic, 19-year-old British nanny, Louise Woodward was found guilty of the second degree murder of one of her charges, baby Mathew Eappen.

The mandatory life sentence – which would have meant Louise serving a minimum 15 years in a tough US jail – caused outraged demands for mercy.

The theatricality of trial-by-TV and the emotional "victim" testimony of Mathew's parents, made gripping viewing, but raised questions about whether justice was being done. Louise's defence team was also blamed for the "all or nothing" tactic of refusing to consider a guilty plea to the lesser charge of manslaughter.

A "Raise the Sapphire" campaign was launched in support of the families of the four fishermen lost in the trawler tragedy.

The Daily Record and Sunday Mail pledged £10,000 – and challenged the Government to match the Scottish donations to help raise the trawler and recover the men's bodies.

TODAY: TENERIFE

WIN A SUPER HOLIDAY A DAY

PAGE 32

HAVE A CRACKING CHRISTMAS ON US!

Token collect

PAGE 26

Blizzard traps poison fumes family

By ALLISON McLAUGHLIN

A FAMILY overcome by killer gas fumes were stranded in a snowbound village last night.

A fleet of ambulances and police teams battled through blizzards to rescue them.

A Navy helicopter was also called into the operation but was forced to abort its mission because of the white-out.

The three adults and two girls, aged four and eight, suffered carbon monoxide poisoning when fumes leaked from the gas heating system at their home in Forth, Lanarkshire.

An ambulance was sent from Motherwell but was trapped behind a lorry stuck in snowdrifts. Other ambulances from Shotts and Livingston tried to reach the village from different directions but couldn't get through either.

Scrambled

Four-wheel-drive Landrover ambulances were then sent to help and one – with a paramedic and vital oxygen on board – eventually reached the family.

But then it couldn't get back out of the village.

A Sea King helicopter from HMS Gannet in Prestwick was scrambled.

The Landrover drove to a nearby field to prepare a landing site and locals used their car headlights to light up the area. But the copter was forced down by heavy snow at Newmains, just 10 miles from Forth.

Police then called out a snowplough to clear the roads and early this morning a JCB was towing the ambulance, with the family onboard, 15 miles through snowdrifts to Law Hospital.

SNOWBOUND – Page Two

BUG SCANDAL: *Cover-up claim as death toll hits six*

BUTCHER SOLD DEADLY MEAT AFTER E COLI WARNING

WARNED ... Butcher John Barr

By TOM LITTLE and ROGER HANNAH

THE butcher at the centre of the E Coli epidemic sold danger meat AFTER health chiefs asked him to stop.

As the death toll from the outbreak rose to six yesterday, officials said John Barr twice promised them he'd withdraw cooked meat from his shop in Wishaw, Lanarkshire.

They had the power to shut him down at that time, but didn't.

Sandwiches

And less than **TWO HOURS** after Mr Barr's second visit from the council, a mum was sold cold meat to make sandwiches for her daughter's 18th birthday party that night.

She says Mr Barr personally assured her the meat was safe.

Mr Barr now faces police questions over the sale of the meat. He and his staff will be interviewed within the next few days.

At least 22 people out of more

TURN TO PAGE SIX

WIN A FAMILY HOLIDAY

TODAY: FLORIDA PAGE 22

DUNBLANE JOY: *Anti-gun song is Britain's biggest-selling single*

WE'RE THE TOPS ... Dunblane families celebrate last night
Picture: RICHARD PARKER

ONE-DERFUL!

Kids are top of the pops

THE Dunblane song stormed to No 1 in the charts last night.

Jubilant kids and adults partied to celebrate the town's hit.

By ROGER HANNAH

They gathered at the home of John and Alison Crozier, parents of massacre victim Emma.

And they let out a huge cheer

when Radio 1 DJ Mark Goodier told the nation their record was top of the pops.

For the first time in a long time the town had a reason to party – and they hugged and **TURN TO PAGE TWO**

28

Daily Record

Friday, December 20, 1996   28p

SCOTLAND'S CHAMPION

SUZANNE'S SANTA SURPRISE
PAGES 32 & 37

TOMORROW CHRISTMAS TV
36-PAGE GUIDE TO ALL YOUR FESTIVE TELLY

WIN A FABULOUS HOLIDAY IN TURKEY   PAGE 42

QUIP ... Duke

Philip knew he had goofed

By JANICE BURNS

LOUDMOUTH Prince Philip knew he'd shot himself in the foot just seconds after an astonishing slur about Dunblane.

The duke said immediately after his pro-guns rant:

"That will really set the cat among the pigeons, won't it?

The 75-year-old duke stunned BBC presenter Rob Bonnet when he made his gaffe.

And yesterday shocked head Ron Taylor said it was "outrageous" for the duke to say gun owners were no more dangerous than golfers or cricketers.

FULL STORY
Pages 4 and 5

ROAD RAGE GIRL ON MURDER CHARGE

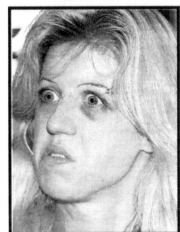

TRACIE ANDREWS ... charged by police

THE fiancee of "road rage victim" Lee Harvey was last night charged with his murder.

Tracie Andrews had been quizzed by police all day yesterday about the stabbing in an isolated country lane.

Andrews, 27, who lived with Lee at a flat in the Worcestershire village of Alvechurch, was charged at 10pm.

Police had arrested her two weeks ago, but were unable to interview her at the time as she was taken to hospital after taking an overdose.

She had faced television cameras just two days after Lee's death in an appeal to catch the killer. Breaking down in tears, she told how

TURN TO PAGE NINE

sunday mail

55p   December 22, 1996   4203

IT'S A CRACKER

Month by month guide to your '97 stars ...by the astrologer to the stars

Santa brings smiles to tragic little Lauren — **Page 28**

WIN A SUPER FAMILY HOLIDAY — See Page 19

The IRA festive calling card...

THE IRA left their Christmas message ... a bullet hole in an incubator at a Belfast children's hospital. Only yards away, youngsters were fighting for life, but that didn't matter to the men of violence.

FULL STORY – Page 5

GEOFF ... TV Don

STREET'S BLACK CHRISTMAS

SUICIDE FEARS OVER SOAP

TELLY BOSSES have been forced to tag a suicide warning on to the end of the Coronation Street Christmas Day blockbuster.

The episode shows a suicide bid by taxi driver Don Brennan in a fume-filled car.

And the soap bosses consulted The Samaritans because they feared viewers

TURN TO PAGE 5

sunday mail

55p December 29, 1996 4204

WIN £1997
Great cash prize for a really happy New Year
Page 31

1997 See into your future with our super stars guide
Page 34

1997 Start the year with a dream family holiday
Page 21

Goalden wonders

£58,000 for Di Canio boots

● THE golden boots of Celtic star Paolo Di Canio have a £58,000 Midas touch. For sports shop boss Tom Hunter yesterday shelled out £30,000 for them in a charity radio auction. He beat Lottery winner John McGuinness, who let his £28,000 offer also go to needy kids.

FULL STORY – Page 3

Di's mum and the Bishop

LAY OFF RODDY

FRIEND ... Mrs Shand Kydd

RUNAWAY ... Roddy Wright

EXCLUSIVE
By JANE FINDLAY

PRINCESS Di's mum yesterday sprang to the defence of shamed ex-bishop Roddy Wright.

Frances Shand Kydd, a long-term pal of randy runaway Roddy, told the *Mail* that she was "totally disgusted" over what she believed were moves to stir up the scandal.

She spoke out after a survey of locals in the former bishop's diocese of Argyll and the Isles.

It asked people for their verdict on Wright, who quit his job to run off with divorcee Kathy MacPhee.

The survey invited anonymous responses on whether Wright, who also fathered a child by another woman, should be allowed to return to the church.

Mrs Shand Kydd, who lives on the Isle of Seil, near Oban, branded the survey

TURN TO PAGE 2

31

TORTURED

Saudi cops made innocent nurse admit to murder

NIGHTMARE ORDEAL ... Monica Hall spent three years in jail

A NURSE told yesterday how Saudi police tortured her into admitting murder.

And Monica Hall said caged Scots girl Lucy McLauchlan may be going through the same hell.

Monica, 46, was made to listen to another prisoner being beaten, guns were held on her, and she was drugged and not allowed to sleep.

After 11 days, she admitted murdering her best friend.

She spent nearly three years in a grim

EXCLUSIVE
By ANNA SMITH

Saudi jail, but insists she was innocent.

Monica now fears for nurse Lucy, 31, of Dundee, and English woman Debbie Parry, 41, who are being held in Saudi Arabia over a colleague's murder.

Sources there say Debbie has admitted the killing and Lucy has confessed to being an accessory. They face public beheadings if found guilty.

Monica told how she cracked under Saudi interrogation in 1986. She said: "In a

TURN TO PAGE FIVE

CHARGE ... Lucy McLauchlan

Daily Record

Wednesday, January 8, 1997   28p

SCOTLAND'S CHAMPION

EXCLUSIVE
KELLY'S CURES!
LORRAINE TRIES OUT DI'S REMEDIES PAGE 20

£150,000
SCOTSCRATCH PAGE 10

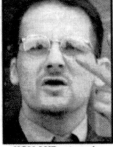

HOLLAND ... transfer

Siege con grabs second woman hostage

A PRISONER was involved in a SECOND jail hostage drama within 24 hours yesterday.

Armed robber James Holland grabbed a young female trainee solicitor soon after he was transferred to Perth Prison.

He held her for 30 minutes in an interview room before prison officers broke down the door and overpowered him.

Holland, 26, was sent to Perth after taking part in a siege at Glenochil Prison, near Alloa, where a female nurse and a prison warder were held.

The solicitor – a single woman in her 20s – was part of the team expected to act for him over the Glenochil incident.

HIV-positive Holland was with her when a warder heard a table being moved in the room and raised the alarm.

Holland, who was cleared of taking part in another hostage-taking three years ago, told warders he had a knife.

Perth Governor Michael Duffy sent for trained negotiators.

But after the lawyer wrote a note saying Holland was armed and making threats, Mr Duffy decided to send in two intervention teams, each made up of three men.

After breaking down the

TURN TO PAGE FIVE

CROWN AND OUT

Scotland votes to get rid of royals

YOU'VE SCOT TO GO... Queen voted out

SCOTLAND voted to kick out the Royal Family last night.

In a huge TV phone poll, 56 per cent said No to the monarchy with 44 per cent backing the Queen.

Scotland was the **ONLY** part of the UK to

By JOHN McEACHRAN

demand the royals be dumped.

Nine other areas voted overwhelmingly to keep them.

Nationally, 66 per cent of Brits were in favour of the monarchy with only 34 per cent against.

A record 2.6million people called the poll – including around 340,000 Scots.

The vote to turn Scotland

into a republic could have been even higher.

Thousands who tried to phone the ITV programme, Monarchy – The Nation Decides, failed to get through as the hotline for No votes was swamped.

Hundreds of angry Scots rang the Record to protest at being unable to register their vote.

It was filmed live in front of a 3000-strong audience in Birmingham. Afterwards, SNP

TURN TO PAGE TWO

sunday mail

55p   January 12, 1997   4206

MAC JACKO

I'll make my home here in Scotland

WACKO Jacko fell in love with Scotland yesterday.

And he revealed his secret trip north was to buy a castle.

In an exclusive interview with the *Mail*, he said: "I love it here in Scotland. I want to make this my home."

At his hotel on the banks of Loch Lomond, Jackson raved about the country – and the Scots.

He said: "The country is beautiful and the people are beautiful."

Megarich Jackson said he wanted to buy a castle and revealed: "I am looking around just now."

He had been on a sightseeing tour of Stirling Castle – but it is NOT for sale.

JACKO TALKS ONLY TO THE SUNDAY MAIL   Pages 4 and 5

EXCLUSIVE

Convict warned of jail kidnap plot...

PAGES 12 and 13

EXCLUSIVE

E-Coli butcher ready to open again

PAGE 7

34

PLAY

£150,000 INSTANT SCRATCH

SCOTSCRATCH INSTANT WIN £150,000

PAGE 26

SCOTTISH PEOPLE'S Film FESTIVAL

MOVIE BONANZA FOR REEL SCOTS

PAGE 22

Fergie's juicy £½m for telly ad

EXCLUSIVE
By JAMES WHITAKER

FERGIE is to appear in a TV advert to help pay off her monstrous debts.

But the health juice commercial won't be shown in Britain because her royal in-laws would choke on it.

And the Duchess of York has admitted to pals that she feels "humiliated" at the lengths she's going to for the £500,000 cheque.

The advert for Cranberry juice is being filmed in Los Angeles today.

Outraged

Fergie thinks the ad – a first for any British royal – would have outraged people in the UK so it will only be shown in the States.

But the way she is cashing in on her title is sure to infuriate Buckingham Palace.

The single mum of two of the Queen's grandchildren believes she can't miss the opportunity to knock a hole in her reported remaining debts of just more than £2million.

A close pal said: "She
TURN TO PAGE NINE

'We've seen Lucy and we know she's innocent'

HUGS AND TEARS IN ARAB JAIL

TOGETHER ... Parents Stan and veiled Ann had an emotional reunion with Lucy

By ANNA SMITH

THE parents of Saudi nurse Lucy McLauchlan last night emerged from her jail and insisted: "Our girl is innocent."

Stan and Ann McLauchlan spent an emotional two hours with Lucy, who's being held on a murder charge.

Mum Ann, 49, wore a headscarf and long tunic for the prison visit.

She was in tears as she hugged her daughter, who has been in jail for nearly a month.

The couple took letters and clothes from home to give to Lucy.

After the visit, dad Stan, 52, said: "She is OK and we were very glad to see her.

"It has reassured us and we
TURN TO PAGE FIVE

Daily Record

Wednesday, January 15, 1997 — 28p

SCOTLAND'S CHAMPION

DALGLISH IS GEORDIE BOSS

KING CANNY SCORES £6M

I'll save war baby vows caring Diana

CARING Di yesterday cuddled a baby in danger of dying during her Red Cross visit to war-torn Angola.

She was deeply moved by Maria Vemba and her two-month-old son.

The princess vowed to do all she could to help the baby, who is desperately ill with a stomach complaint.

Maria said: "The lady said she would help my son live. She promised money and medication. I owe her so much. She is so good."

Di also met people maimed by landmines in the African state's civil war.

SUPPORTING ROLE PAGES 2 and 3

KENNY DALGLISH became the £6million man last night after he took over as boss of Newcastle United.

The canny Scot will be the highest-paid football manager in Britain after negotiating a pay deal worth £23,000 **A WEEK**.

King Kenny, 45, a former apprentice joiner from Glasgow, is already a multi-millionaire.

His sensational return to manage-

TALK OF THE TOON
PAGES 46, 47 and 48

ment has earned him a contract worth £1million a year. On top of that, the former Celtic legend has landed a megabucks share option deal.

Newcastle fans – nicknamed the Toon Army – welcomed Dalglish's decision to replace Kevin Keegan.

Kenny said last night: "I will do my best to achieve what they want."

But the appointment was bad news for Rangers.

It means Dalglish will have to pull out of his £150,000-a-year deal with Ibrox

TURN TO PAGE TWO

KING OF THE CASTLE ... Dalglish yesterday

Daily Record

Wednesday, January 22, 1997 — 28p

SCOTLAND'S CHAMPION

EXCLUSIVE
BITTER SWEET BIG YIN
BOB SHIELDS SPECIAL PAGE 22

Peers blow hole in Tories' pistol purge

By CLARE HOLLAND

REBEL Tory peers blew a huge hole in the Government's gun laws yesterday.

They humiliated John Major with his **THIRD** defeat in the House of Lords in two days.

Major's Westminster misery hit a new low as the Lords backed more compensation for gun club owners threatened by the crackdown.

The Tories have already agreed to a package worth around £150million.

And last night, the Home Office warned the defeat could cost taxpayers a fortune.

Beating

Peers followed up their double victory over police bugging powers by handing the Prime Minister a 158 votes to 135 cuffing.

Tory lords, angered by the attack on their gun-toting traditions, ignored Government warnings that the public wouldn't take it.

Anti-gun campaigners were outraged by the Lords vote.

Ann Pearston, of the Snowdrop Campaign, said: "I would rather this money was spent on anything else but gun clubs.

"It would be much better spent on school security, the health service or buying books

TURN TO PAGE TWO

FRAMED
Jailed Lucy set up on Saudi murder rap says former nurse

By ANNA SMITH

THE Scots nurse facing a Saudi murder charge has been framed, it was claimed yesterday.

And the real killer may still be stalking the hospital complex where **TWO** nurses have been bludgeoned to death.

An Australian woman, who worked there for two years, said Lucy McLauchlan, of Dundee, and a colleague from England had been stitched up over the murder of Yvonne Gilford.

Sharon Markula told the Record: "Two nurses have been killed in identical circumstances. I believe the killer is still at large."

Her pal was robbed and beaten to death in 1994.

Sharon said: "It has to be the same person who's responsible. Yvonne's death is like a copycat killing."

CHARGED ... nurse Lucy

FULL STORY ~ Pages 4 & 5

SET-UP CLAIM ... Sharon Markula

Daily Record

Saturday, January 25, 1997   28p

SCOTLAND'S CHAMPION

2 FREE
GOES ON THE £10 MILLION
LOTTO

SEE PAGE 54

Scots babes sick in milk poison scare

By TOM LITTLE

FOUR Scots babies have been struck down by a food bug linked to a brand of baby milk.

The tots fell victim to salmonella after they were bottle-fed with powdered milk.

It's believed the brand – Milumil – is regularly fed to 25,000 babies across the UK.

Government health chiefs ordered shops nationwide to remove thousands of boxes of the French-made milk powder from the shelves yesterday.

Warned

Makers Milupa halted production and set up a helpline.

They also pledged not to start selling the milk again until they were sure it was safe.

Medics were told to watch out for cases and parents were warned to stop using the powder.

The shock moves came after tests showed 10 out of 12 victims of a rare form of salmonella were fed with Milumil.

The feed is for babies under 12 months old and the alert affects around one in 30 of them.

All four Scots babies are understood to have recovered fully.

BUG ALERT
Pages 6 and 7

Lucky Elaine is our £100,000 winner

Picture: WILLIAM THORNTON

WHEEL OF FORTUNE!

EXCLUSIVE
By MARGARET MALLON

LUCKY Elaine Thomson is living life in the fast lane after scooping the Record's £100,000.

The 26-year-old burst into tears of joy yesterday when we surprised her with news of her fortune.

She cracked open a bottle of bubbly and vowed to splash her cash – then tried out a speedy MGF sports car.

Her husband, John, 30, added: "Now we'll be able to afford the house of our dreams!"

FULL STORY ~ Pages 2 and 3

£150,000 INSTANT SCRATCH
PAGE 48

Rangers Goldfinger, the Celtic director... and £9.4m scandal

JOE LEWIS... Rangers billionaire

DERMOT DESMOND... £9.4m probe

EXCLUSIVE

RANGERS' new Goldfinger investor Joe Lewis had close business links with a top Celtic director. And we can reveal the Parkhead board member Dermot Desmond has figured in a £9.4million land deal scandal.

One of the shareholders listed in the company at the time of the 1991 probe was Mr Lewis, who owned 2.5 per cent. The affair led to an official inquiry which named Desmond as the man who controlled the deal.

And we can also reveal that, in April, Mr Lewis will be named as Britain's richest man with a fortune totalling £3 billion.

FULL STORY... Page 5

Daily Record

Friday, February 7, 1997 — 28p

SCOTLAND'S CHAMPION

7 in new E Coli scare

By JANICE BURNS

SCOTLAND was rocked last night by a new outbreak of the killer E Coli bug.

Health chiefs in Tayside revealed the bacteria is the same strain which has killed 19 people in Lanarkshire.

Seven people are suffering from the new bug – but only three are in hospital.

A spokesman for Tayside Health Board said: "Three patients suffering from E Coli poisoning have been admitted to the infectious diseases unit of Kings Cross Hospital in Dundee.

Concern

"All are suffering from E Coli 0157 – the same strain that struck in Lanarkshire.

"One of the patients is giving serious cause for concern."

Five of the victims are from the same nursing home.

Eighteen people died after Britain's biggest E Coli outbreak hit Lanarkshire two months ago.

The scare was

TURN TO PAGE NINE

CLUCKY!

Chicken couple scoop lottery £3.3m

WHEN ONE BECOMES 2

CHUBBY Spice Girl Geri Halliwell pulled on a Comic Relief red nose yesterday – and ended up looking like Miss Piggy.

The former topless model has shocked fans by piling on the pounds in recent weeks. Now she's hoping to pile on the £s for Comic Relief.

The girl group are donating all royalties from their new single Who Do You Think You Are?

By BRIAN McCARTNEY

A SCOTS couple who work at a chicken farm won £3.3million in the first Winsday lotto draw.

But Bill and Margaret Watson were still up before dawn yesterday morning to feed the hens.

And they told their boss they won't quit their seven-day-a-week jobs.

Margaret, 55, and Bill, 58, have worked at Grange Poultry farm near their home in Errol, Perthshire, for 30 years.

They bought their ticket in the local Spar shop, and saw

TURN TO PAGE FIVE

Daily Record

Tuesday, February 11, 1997   28p

SCOTLAND'S CHAMPION

TODAY & EVERY TUESDAY

FREE PROPERTY GUIDE

Home RECORD

36 PAGE SPECIAL

PLUS: WIN A £100,000 DREAM HOME

RECORD CAMPAIGN: *Victory as Lords back down over new law*

GUNS BAN IN THREE WEEKS

LORD McINTOSH

EXCLUSIVE
By BRENDAN MURPHY

A BAN on 200,000 handguns will become law within three weeks, the Record can reveal today.

Tory peers who schemed to sabotage the new Firearms Bill have now told Labour's Lord McIntosh they will give it a "free run".

He said he was "overjoyed" by the news and

TURN TO PAGE FOUR

ORDER ... Simpson

OJ must fork out another $25m

OJ SIMPSON was yesterday ordered to pay out $25million over the killings of his ex-wife and her friend.

A jury decided that's what he should fork out as punitive damages for the double slaying.

The judgment was on top of the $8.5million he was ordered to pay last week as compensation for the families of Nicole Brown and Ronald Goldman.

The civil case in Santa Monica, California, is an astonishing turnaround from Simpson's shock acquittal on the double murder rap in October

TURN TO PAGE 3

Daily Record

Thursday, February 13, 1997   28p

SCOTLAND'S CHAMPION

WIN A £100,000 DREAM HOUSE

PAGE 36

Fergie swears at fans

TARTAN Army fans last night accused Scotland star Ian Ferguson of SWEARING at them after the 0-0 flop against Estonia.

The Rangers midfielder lashed out at the Scots supporters who made the trek to Monaco, after they showed their frustration by booing the team.

As centre-half Colin Calderwood applauded the Tartan Army, Ferguson snapped: "Don't clap them ... *****."

Ferguson claims the foul-mouthed outburst, caught on TV, was aimed at the Estonian players 40 yards away.

But raging Scots fans jammed the Record switchboard with complaints about him.

SEE BACK PAGE

Jacko wife in labour

SUPERSTAR Michael Jackson was waiting to become a father last night after his wife went into labour.

Debbie Rowe, 37, was secretly admitted to Cedars Sinai Medical Hospital in Beverly Hills yesterday afternoon.

Jacko's former nurse was a week premature, but was given drugs to bring on labour.

Some New York newspapers claimed the birth was being induced to fit in with Jacko's tight schedule.

Debbie will spend less than a week with the child before handing it over to Jacko, 38, and going back to her normal life.

It's thought she

TURN TO PAGE 3

A LIGHT TO REMEMBER

1m candle tribute for Dunblane

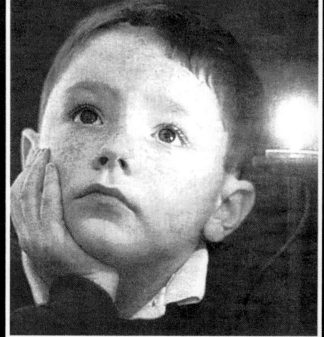

MARK OF RESPECT ... little Stewart Weir remembers his pals

THE Daily Record today asks all Scots to join the parents of Dunblane by lighting a candle on the first anniversary of the tragedy.

We will give away **ONE MILLION** candles to readers before the tribute on March 13.

Stewart Weir, six, who was

By ALLISON McLAUGHLIN

injured in the shootings, lit the first one last night.

The relatives of the dead – 16 infant schoolchildren and their teacher Gwen Mayor – have decided to light candles as their own show of respect.

And they would love to see a tiny flame shining from every home in the country.

LIGHT UP SCOTLAND~ Pages 4 & 5

Daily Record

Monday, February 17, 1997   28p

SCOTLAND'S CHAMPION

HIGHWAY ROBBERY
Spanish charge truckers £2.50 for a wash

EXCLUSIVE
By ROGER HANNAH

SCOTS truckers stranded by a lorry strike in Spain are being charged £2.50 for water to wash in.

The desperate drivers, almost penniless after being trapped for five days, can't afford the highway robbery prices.

Chic Lavelle, 51, from Motherwell, said: "We can either eat or wash.

"We're stuck with no facilities and the only hotel around here is ripping us off.

"It's 500 pesetas for a wash – about £2.50.

"Why spend that on a wash when it can get you a loaf or a bit of cheese?"

"We're going about like tramps, not washing or shaving."

Grandad Chic was stopped by pickets on Wednesday and hasn't moved since.

He is one of five Scots being held with 1500 other non-Spanish drivers on an industrial estate in Burgos, 150 miles north of Madrid.

Other groups of truckers are trapped elsewhere in Spain.

Stranded Britons say drivers have been threatened with baseball bats and even shot at for trying to get through the blockade. Strikers have also smashed lorry windscreens and slashed tyres.

"I've got a cracked windscreen," said Chic. The pickets are just throwing

TURN TO PAGE TWO

DESPERATE ... Chic Lavelle

EWAN'S TOP OF THE SCOTS
FULL STORY ~ Page 18

PLAY £150,000 INSTANT SCRATCH
PAGE 22

STARTS ON SATURDAY

3 DAYS TO PAYDAY

PICK UP A PACKET!

£10,000

TO BE WON EVERY WEEK

PIES GUYS

Rangers hand out free grub

EXCLUSIVE
By CARA PAGE

RANGERS last night gave away thousands of free pies after their match at Ibrox was rained off.

The club handed them out to centres for homeless people across Glasgow.

Frank Weldon, who lives at a Salvation Army hostel, said: "I'm a Celtic fan but this shows Rangers can't be all bad."

Ibrox was ready to feed 48,000 fans for the game against Dundee United.

And £3000 worth of food had already arrived when the match was cancelled.

Catering boss Peter Kingston said: "It wouldn't have kept until our next home game on Sunday.

"And we just don't

TURN TO PAGE 11

CAMERON WINS GOLD

Crippled track star in line for £2m payout

VICTORY ... Cameron with wife Carol and daughters Lynsey, 6, and Carly, 9,

CRIPPLED sprint star Cameron Sharp won his five-year battle for damages yesterday.

Health chiefs finally admitted leaving Cameron, 38, a mental and physical wreck by taking too long to realise he needed brain surgery after a road crash.

Dad of two Cameron, a Commonwealth Games gold medallist for Scotland, is in line for a payout of almost £2million.

FULL STORY-Pages 2 and 3

PLAY £150,000 SCOTSCRATCH

PAGE 42

STARTS TODAY

£10,000 TO BE WON

3 DAYS TO PAYDAY

PAGE 56

2 FREE GOES ON LOTTERY!

PAGE 34

CHANCE **A**

. 03 09 19 21 34 49

CHANCE **B**

07 11 13 28 32 48

CRY FREEDOM

BRIDGEWA

Tears as 3 leave jail after 19 years

AGONY OVER ... Jim Robinson, left, weeps with joy, above, Vincent and Michael Hickey

KISSING GOODBYE TO PRISON HELL
Pages 2 and 3

Daily Record

Tuesday, February 25, 1997   28p

SCOTLAND'S CHAMPION

Help save our kids from perverts

SCOTLAND'S CHILD ABUSE SCANDAL

AGONY ... Thousands suffer in silence *(Posed by model)*

BY THE EDITOR

THE Daily Record today reveals Scotland's child abuse shame – and calls for urgent action to protect our youngsters from perverts.

In a series that will shock every parent, we reveal ...

● How one in five girls and one in 14 boys are at risk from adults;

● How 19 out of 20 paedophiles are never brought to justice;

● And how sex beasts are released without controls – often to re-offend.

Astonishingly, nobody knows exactly how many children are victims because there are no official records.

Yet the SSPCA can tell us how many **ANIMALS** were abused last year. It is a

TURN TO PAGE TWO

DAILY RECORD

CHARTER FOR OUR CHILDREN

● **PERVERTS' PLAYGROUND:** Pages 2 & 3

● **GALLERY OF SHAME:** Pages 4 and 5

● **END OUR CHILDREN'S SUFFERING:** Page 8

● **MONSTER FREED TO KILL:** Pages 22 & 27

Daily Record

Wednesday, February 26, 1997   28p

SCOTLAND'S CHAMPION

SCOTLAND'S VICTIMS BACK OUR BID TO STOP PERVERTS

'It may be too late for me .. but if you save one child it will be worth it'

POSED BY MODEL

By ROGER HANNAH

SCOTLAND yesterday backed the Record's campaign to save our children from perverts.

Thousands of Scots – many victims of abuse – jammed our telephone hotline.

Some wept as they praised our charter to protect youngsters from paedophiles

One victim sobbed: "It may be too late for me but if you can save just one child from going through what I did, it will be worth it."

Another caller revealed she still had nighmares about abuse she suffered SIXTY years ago.

She said: "It never really goes away. I am a pensioner and it's still in my mind."

MPs also voiced support for the Record's eight-point Charter For Our Children.

Yesterday, we told how one in five girls and one in 14 boys are at risk from adults. We pointed out how 19 out of 20 paedophiles are never brought to justice.

And we revealed how there are **NO** official records for victims of child abuse – yet there **ARE** detailed statistics on animal abuse.

Labour's Scottish home affairs spokesman John McFall immediately tabled Commons questions to Scottish Office ministers about the lack of information on child abuse cases and

TURN TO PAGE 2

CHARTER FOR OUR CHILDREN: Pages 6, 7, 8, 9, 22 & 27

Perverts target single mothers

By JOAN BURNIE

PAEDOPHILES are using lonely hearts ads to get at the children of vulnerable single mothers.

The perverts scour the adverts for targets, worm their way into the women's confidence, then start abusing their children.

Some even go as far as marrying the mums.

The problem topped the agenda this week at a conference of senior police from throughout Scotland.

Three mums told the Record yesterday how perverts they met through small ads preyed on their kids and ruined their lives.

We have used false names to protect the families affected.

Widow Susan married the man she

DAILY RECORD

CHARTER FOR OUR CHILDREN

met, and he abused her five-year-old son.

She said: "My only crime was being lonely.

"After my son was attacked, I found out my husband had 21 child abuse convictions."

Fellow-victim Irene said: "Lots of women who suffer like this blame themselves.

"Lonely hearts columns and dating agencies are accepted and widespread, yet there are no safeguards."

Single mum Liz answered an ad from a man who wrote: "Children are a positive asset."

She later discovered he was interfering with her youngest son.

Liz said: "I was falling in love with this man, but I ended up trying to throw boiling water over his private parts."

The pressure group One Parent Families

TURN TO PAGE TWO

CAMPAIGN SPECIAL
Pages 10, 11, 12 and 13

HEART OP AGONY OF BILLY McNEILL

SHOCK... Billy yesterday

SOCCER legend Billy McNeill is to undergo a major heart op.

The former Celtic and Scotland star will have emergency surgery next week.

The operation on the Lisbon

By BILL CAVEN

Lion could be as early as Monday – the day after his 57th birthday.

Last night Billy looked tired and drawn at the door of his home.

But the man dubbed "Caesar" by the Parkhead fans, was defiant about his illness and vowed: "I'll be back

brand new. I would love to play football again some day.

"But I don't know too much about what is going to happen."

It's understood the soccer great will undergo a triple bypass operation to remedy hardening of the arteries.

Billy, who lives in Newlands in the

TURN TO PAGE FIVE

THE CELTIC FOOTBALL CLUB 1888

WIN £100,000 DREAM HOME
PAGE 43

MAJOR WIPED OUT IN TORY STRONGHOLD

LABOUR POWER HOME!

TRIUMPH ... Blair

DESPAIR ... Major

RAUNCHY ... Geri

SCOT AND SPICY

EXCLUSIVE
By JOHN DINGWALL

THE Spice Girls are heading to Scotland with their raunchy show.

Geri, Emma, Mel B, Mel C and Victoria are embarking on their first-ever live tour.

And they want to include at least one Scottish date among a string of concerts lined up for September.

The gigs are sure to be instant sell-outs and will include new stage versions of their hits Wannabe, Say You'll Be There and 2 Become 1.

Mel C said: "We've got a lot

TURN TO PAGE THREE

TRIUMPHANT Tony Blair last night powered to a historic by-election victory.

The Tory stronghold of Wirral South voted to ditch John Major and his desperate Government.

By NIGEL MORRIS

And it sent a clear message that Britain wants Tony Blair as Prime Minister.

Labour's Ben Chapman stormed to a 7888-vote majority, leaving Major clinging to power by his fingertips.

His minority Government is now

outgunned in the Commons by 323 MPs to 322.

But he is still likely to hang on to office until his favoured May 1 General Election showdown.

After the result, delighted Labour leader Blair said: "The people of Wirral have had the chance to vote. Now the whole country wants that chance.

"The Tories can dismiss this as a

TURN TO PAGE TWO

sunday mail

55p   March 2, 1997   4213

GLITTER
Street star's fashion secrets

BITTER
How Kim lost £10m fortune

Tories try to gag the *sunday mail*

■ **ARROGANT** Tory big-wigs tried to slap a ban on the *Sunday Mail*. They attempted to gag us from reporting on their pre-election bash in Glasgow attended by despairing John Major.

The tottering Tories were worried stiff that we would tell the truth about what went on at the "party for the party" attended by 1,200 activists on the banks of the Clyde.

They sent an invitation to the *Sunday Mail* a week ago.

But on Friday – the day after they

Turn to Page 2

BABY PLUCKED FROM SEA!

LOCAL HERO ... Alex Grieve waded in to help

A BABY boy was brought back to life after he and his mum were plucked from icy, storm-lashed seas.

The child almost lost his life when the pair fell into a harbour lashed by gale force winds.

But he was saved after passers-by saw him floating face down in the water and two heroic rescuers battled the huge waves.

Eddie Paterson, 41, waded up to his neck into the freezing water to save the baby.

After the pipefitter dragged the boy onto dry land, he thumped the lifeless child's back to restart his breathing.

He was joined in the rescue by lorry driver Alex Grieve, 35, who raced the baby to a nearby bakery to warm him up.

Alex then returned to the water to help the 44-year-old mother as bakery staff Anne

Turn to Page 7

50

Daily Record

Saturday, March 8, 1997   FIRST   28p

SCOTLAND'S CHAMPION

LORRAINE KELLY

ME AND MY MUM

Pages 20,21

2 FREE GOES ON THE LOTTO

PAGE 69

CHANCE A   .07 24 34 38 47 49

CHANCE B   19 20 30 35 36 48

March 9

Blair's on the ball!

TONY BLAIR warms up to tackle the Tories at the polls by enjoying a kick-about with soccer-daft kids yesterday. The Labour leader was in Inverness before speaking at the Scots Labour Party conference.

LION TAMER-PAGES 2 AND 3

GIRL, 14 HELD IN CELL FOR 2 DAYS

By GRACE MCLEAN

A GIRL of 14 was left in a police cell for 48 HOURS.

Furious MPs and civil liberties groups last night demanded an explanation for the youngster's ordeal.

The girl, who is in care, TURN TO PAGE SEVEN

Daily Record

Monday, March 10, 1997   28p

SCOTLAND'S CHAMPION

MONEY MONEY MONDAY

3 DAYS TO PAY DAY

Token 3 page 29

Wizard of Oz

FLYING Scot David Coulthard scorched his way to victory in the Australian Grand Prix yesterday.

And last night his dad revealed the secret behind Braveheart David's great win.

The Monaco-based supercar superstar had forgotten to buy a Mother's Day present!

Sheepish David, 25, called his parents hours before his greatest-ever triumph and admitted the mishap.

But mum Joyce eased the

TURN TO PAGE TWO

HEARTACHE: *Little Rowan, 2, fights for life*

NANNY'S PRAYERS FOR MURIEL'S BABY

By TONY ELLIN

THE NANNY of TV star Muriel Gray's tragic daughter said last night: "I'm praying to God for her life."

It is feared Rowan, two, may have brain damage after almost drowning in a garden pond.

Muriel was keeping an all-night vigil at Rowan's bedside. Nanny Veronica Maguire was in charge of the tot and Muriel's son Hector, four, when the freak accident happened.

In tears, she said: "I want people to know I'm thinking of the little one.

"We are all willing her to pull through."

Rowan was found face down

TURN TO PAGE FOUR

Daily Record

Tuesday, March 11, 1997   28p

SCOTLAND'S CHAMPION

Fiend freed to strike again

By RAY NOTARANGELO

A SERIAL child sex beast walked free TWICE to strike again.

Last night there was outrage as it was revealed two of the kids should never have become victims.

The Daily Record's Charter For Our Children could have helped snare James Robertson before he struck again.

Pervert Robertson, 26, now faces life in jail after his **THIRD** attack on innocent little girls.

Robertson walked free from court in 1992 with probation after his first assault.

He carried out the terrifying attack after binding his little victim with a tie.

A year later, Robertson was jailed for just **SIX MONTHS** after a second sickening child assault.

He partially stripped a seven-year-old girl at knifepoint.

Then he blindfolded his little victim, tied her up and forced her into a cupboard.

Yesterday, at the High Court in Edinburgh, Robertson admitted abducting a seven-year-old girl with intent to commit a sex act and binding and gagging her.

Prosecuting, QC Kevin

TURN TO PAGE FIVE

Four dead after boat sinks

By ALLISON McLAUGHLIN

FOUR men were feared dead last night after a trawler was lost in the North Sea.

The Westhaven and her crew were still missing more than 14 hours after a Mayday call was picked up.

A massive air and sea search was under way early today off the coast of Peterhead.

But hopes were fading after debris was spotted in calm seas near the Piper oilfield 100 miles off Aberdeen.

The 65ft Westhaven left Arbroath, where she was based, early yesterday.

Signal

The rescue operation began shortly after 11am when Falmouth Coastguard picked up a satellite signal from an emergency beacon.

Offshore patrol vessel HMS Guernsey from the Fisheries Protection Squadron and six other vessels were drafted in.

A helicopter was also scouring the sea for the men who all come from Arbroath.

The Guernsey located the beacon but could find no trace of the trawler.

Early this morning an Aberdeen coastguard said: "We are conducting a search for a fishing boat which is well overdue.

"We have very grave concerns for the boat."

RIPPER IS STABBED IN EYES

By ADRIAN SHAW

THE Yorkshire Ripper was last night stabbed in the eyes by a crazed beast known as The Devil.

Evil Peter Sutcliffe was attacked by Woolworth's killer Ian Kay with a fibre-tip pen.

Nurses raced to Sutcliffe's rescue

TURN TO PAGE SIX

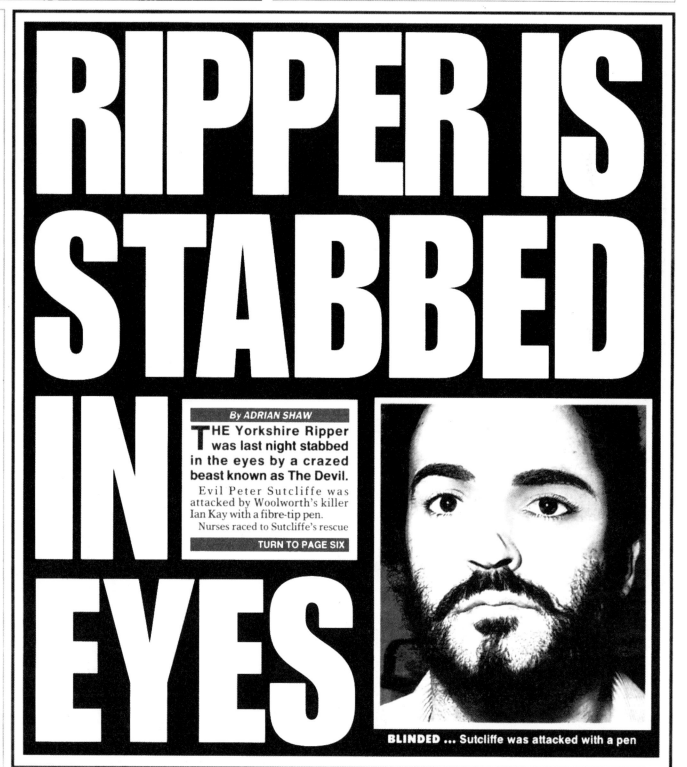

BLINDED ... Sutcliffe was attacked with a pen

LIGHT YOUR CANDLE FOR DUNBLANE

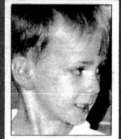

KEVIN

DAVID

CHARLOTTE

EMILY

JOANNA

EMMA

ABIGAIL

SOPHIE

HANNAH

MEGAN

MHAIRI

BRETT

WE'LL NEVER FORGET ... the Dunblane Primary One class and their brave teacher will be remembered in a candlelight vigil throughout Scotland tonight

GWEN

ROSS

JOHN

MELISSA

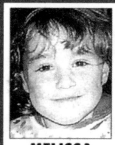

VICTORIA

REMEMBER THE INNOCENTS

TODAY the Daily Record asks all of Scotland to join with the parents of Dunblane and light a candle in a window of your home at 7pm.

This simple, touching tribute is Scotland's way of showing we will never forget the 16 innocent children and their teacher who lost their lives in the tragedy that shocked the world one year ago today.

INSIDE: 16-PAGE DUNBLANE MEMORIAL SUPPLEMENT

Daily Record

Friday, March 14, 1997 28p

SCOTLAND'S CHAMPION

7 SHOT DEAD ON ISLE OF PEACE

● A crazed Arab soldier gunned down seven schoolgirls yesterday in a chilling echo of Dunblane

Full story pages 4 and 5

SCOTLAND'S TRIBUTE TO INNOCENTS OF DUNBLANE

NOT FORGOTTEN ... two Edinburgh teenagers light a candle in last night's tribute to the Dunblane innocents

PICTURE: IAN TORRANCE

SHINING EXAMPLE

By ALLISON McLAUGHLIN

SCOTLAND set a shining example of love last night to honour the dead of Dunblane.

Millions of candles were lit across the nation in a dignified and deeply touching tribute to the sixteen infant schoolchildren and their teacher who died on March 13, 1996.

As Scotland remembered the tragedy a year ago, families in Israel were torn apart by grief.

A demented Arab soldier fired on a party of schoolgirls, killing seven of them.

MILLIONS OF CANDLES LIGHT UP THE NATION - *Full Story Pages 2 & 3*

Daily Record

Tuesday, March 18, 1997　　　28p

LABOUR'S CHAMPION

Record backs Blair's new Britain on May 1

WE'LL WIN IT TOGETHER

ON THE RIGHT TRACK Labour leader Tony Blair and wife Cherie yesterday

IN 44 days Britain will elect a new government for the new century.

The Daily Record believes there is only one choice that's best for Britain and best for Scotland — New Labour.

Through 18 long years of Opposition, the Record has kept faith with Labour. Now Tony Blair and New Labour will keep faith with Scotland.

Together we are an unstoppable

TURN TO PAGE SIX

44 DAYS TO MAJOR'S MAYDAY ~ *Pages 2 & 3* ● **I'LL LEAD BETTER BRITAIN VOWS BLAIR** ~ *Pages 4 & 5*

56

Daily Record

Tuesday, March 25, 1997

SCOTLAND'S CHAMPION

28p

36-PAGE PROPERTY GUIDE

Home RECORD

FREE INSIDE

THE GAME YOU WANNA PLAY!

54321

WIN £10,000 EVERY WEEK

Token on Page 20

OUT FOR THE COUNT: *Link to married blonde finishes Stewart*

TORY MP QUITS OVER SECRET FRIEND

By VIVIENNE AITKEN

TORY MP Allan Stewart quit late last night after reports of his friendship with a married blonde.

The ex-minister blamed the links to Catherine "Bunny" Knight and press reports on his booze problems, saying they had caused "great family distress and personal strain".

His decision not to fight the May 1 election stunned officials in his Eastwood constituency near Glasgow – Scotland's safest Tory seat.

Observers said it turned the seat into a real Labour target.

Ian Muir, chairman of the Eastwood Tory party, called the resignation "a huge tragedy".

He denied Stewart had been pushed, and said the decision was made purely on health grounds. He added: "Allan has

TURN TO PAGE 3

Daily Record

Friday, March 28, 1997   28p

SCOTLAND'S CHAMPION

ROAD RECORD ▶▶ **40-PAGE MOTORS EXTRA!**

TOMORROW

16 FREE SCRATCHCARDS

SCOTSCRATCH INSTANT WIN

PSYCHO...but McGinlay was let out

FREED TO KILL

By PETER LAING

A MURDERER killed for a second time – just hours after being let out of jail on weekend leave.

Evil Joe McGinlay butchered pretty Amanda Barnett with a knife in her flat.

He was jailed for at least another 30 years yesterday as the Scottish Prison Service faced furious demands for an inquiry into why the psycho was let out to kill again.

Leading the calls were Amanda's parents

TURN TO PAGE TWO

SNAPPED: *Tory taken to psychiatric hospital*

SHAMED MP ALLAN BREAKS DOWN

STRESS ... Allan Stewart

By ANNA SMITH and VIVIENNE AITKEN

SHAMED Tory MP Allan Stewart was rushed to hospital yesterday after a nervous breakdown at his home.

Police and ambulances were called when he was seen shouting and screaming in the garden.

Last night Stewart's wife was by his

TURN TO PAGE SEVEN

sunday mail

55p   *March 30, 1997*   4127

BIRTHDAY BLUES FOR Mr MAJOR

GAY SEX SECRETS SINK TOP TORY

TOP Tory Sir Michael Hirst sensationally quit yesterday over a gay sex scandal.

The 51-year-old chairman of the Scots Tory Party fled into hiding after revealing his decision in a bombshell letter to John Major.

Hirst, a father-of-three, admitted to "past indiscretion in my private life" and told Major: "I am desolated to have failed you and my colleagues at such a vital time."

The latest scandal has left Major – whose 54th

TURN TO PAGE TWO

FALL OF THE TORY EMPIRE

Pages 2, 3, 4, 5 and 10

£10,000 MUST BE WON

5 4 3 2 1

PAGES 30 and 31

RACING SPECIAL
16 CARDS IN SCOTLAND'S TOP GUIDE

PLUS: MONEY MONEY MONDAY

EXCLUSIVE: *Party took no action over chairman's TWO affairs*

SCANDAL
Tory top brass covered up for gay-shame Hirst

MISSING ... Forsyth

Knives out for silent Forsyth

By DAVE KING

TOP Tories last night put the boot into Michael Forsyth for dodging the latest sleaze crisis.

They're furious that the Scots Secretary has done a vanishing act as the party tears itself apart over a series of scandals.

And they warned Forsyth's lack of leadership could affect his entire political future.

He is almost certain to be defeated in his Stirling seat because his 700 majority at the last election will be wiped out by boundary changes.

But he is being warned he will not be made welcome in any other Scottish constituency if he seeks a quick return to

TURN TO PAGE 3

By ANNA SMITH, Chief Reporter

TORY top brass covered up the gay double-life of shamed chairman Sir Michael Hirst.

Former Scots Secretary Ian Lang knew about his homosexual affairs with TWO young Tories.

But he took no action after Hirst

TURN TO PAGE TWO

LANG ... he knew

60

Daily Record

Saturday, April 5, 1997   28p

SCOTLAND'S CHAMPION

2 **FREE GOES ON THE LOTTERY** PAGE 33

CHANCE A	CHANCE B
23 32 35 38 39 41	01 02 11 23 31 35

APRIL 5

Tony walks the devo tightrope

A CONFIDENT Tony Blair arrived hand-in-hand with wife Cherie to launch Labour's Scottish manifesto yesterday – but he ended up facing a whirlwind of questions.

Devolution dogged the Labour leader as he sought to clarify the party's pledge over tax-raising powers for a Scottish parliament.

Time and time again he had to repeat they would be available – but Labour would not use them.

But after a tough time Blair came out smiling – convinced he'd unravelled the tartan tangle in time for polling day.

TARTAN TANGLE ~ Pages 4 & 5

£75M ON NATIONAL   £63M ON LOTTO   £20M ON POOLS

YOU BET £190m!

TOP TIPSTER ... jockey Willie Carson opens a Fife bookies yesterday

BRITAIN will go on a record-breaking £190million betting frenzy today.

That's equivalent to **EVERY** person in the country staking almost £4 a head.

And £30million of the cash is expected to come from Scotland.

Bookies reckon British punters will splash out £75million on our

£4 a head in biggest ever punt

By ROGER HANNAH

favourite flutter, the Grand National.

Another £63million will be gambled on tonight's National Lottery draw.

And we'll fork out

TURN TO PAGE TWO

PLAY £10,000 3 DAYS TO PAYDAY
PAGE 32

sunday mail

55p   April 6, 1997   4128

PANIC AS THE IRA TARGET THE BIGGEST RACE IN THE WORLD

NATIONAL DISGRACE

THIS is the moment when one of the world's greatest sporting events was brought to its knees.

The moment when the starter should have been raising his flag to start the Grand National.

Instead, the only horse to be seen as thousands of people fled Aintree after an IRA bomb warning was a mounted police horse.

The famous stands should have been packed with thousands of cheering punters. But many were reduced to tears, including top trainer Jenny Pitman.

TEARS...Pitman

There was only desolation and despair as the National was abandoned ...

Last night thousands of Scots were stranded at Aintree in the chaotic aftermath.

● EVIL OF THE IRA - Page 2   ● MEN OF HATE - Page 12   ● CRYING SHAME - Pages 36 and 37

Daily Record

Tuesday, April 8, 1997   28p

SCOTLAND'S CHAMPION

WE'RE WED FOR IT

PAGES 4 AND 5

Pregnant mum is killed in road smash

By STUART GRIFFITHS

A PREGNANT mum died and her little son was fighting for life after a smash with a lorry yesterday.

Last night, her fiance was in shock at the death of his girlfriend and their unborn baby and praying the boy would pull through.

Five-year-old Kris was with his mum, Debbie Sommerville, 23, when she was in the crash with a 20-ton lorry on a notorious bend in Bellshill, Lanarkshire.

Debbie, of Airdrie, died along with her unborn baby later in hospital.

Loving

Last night, Kris was "very serious" in Glasgow's Southern General Hospital with head injuries.

Debbie, her fiance, David, and Kris were due to move into a new home in Bellshill that they had been preparing.

They were returning to Airdrie in separate cars when tragedy struck.

Her family said they were too upset to talk last night.

Debbie's neighbours paid tribute to the loving mum.

Thomas Woods, 31, said: "It is a tragedy. No one here can take in what happened.

"Debbie was such a careful driver, especially when Kris was in the car."

His mother Margaret, 59, added: "Debbie was three months on in her pregnancy."

The family had planned a fresh start and enrolled Kris at a new school.

FULL STORY
PAGE SEVEN

GRAND DAY OUT: *20,000 defiant punters save the National*

GRINNER ... crowd cheers Tony Dobbin

A WINNER BY SMILES

By MARK McGIVERN

TWENTY thousand punters defied the IRA yesterday to make the Grand National a winner by smiles.

And first past the grinning post was victorious Irish jockey Tony Dobbin, who romped home on Lord Gyllene at 14-1.

It was an incredible day as the huge crowd turned the delayed race into a massive free carnival.

They were joined at Aintree by Princess Anne, who was among the 60,000 evacuated after the big race was

TURN TO PAGE TWO

Daily Record

Saturday, April 12, 1997　　28p

SCOTLAND'S CHAMPION

PLAY TODAY

8 FREE SCRATCH CARDS INSIDE!

5 FREE GOES ON TONIGHT'S LOTTO PAGE 28

CHANCE **A**	CHANCE **B**
APRIL 12	
09 22 25 26 37 47	01 11 19 22 24 33

SARAH... brilliant

Suicide student feared exams

A STAR student has hanged herself because she was terrified over her exams.

Sarah Napuk's tutors expected her to stroll through her Oxford University finals and get a first-class honours degree.

But Sarah, 22, of Edinburgh, was haunted by the fear of failing to meet her own high standards at the exams in six weeks time.

Pals said she'd been having counselling for severe stress brought on by her studies.

Ironically, she spent some of her time at Oxford advising other students with problems.

History student Sarah was found hanged in her rented house on Thursday afternoon by her fiance Jason Russell.

One of her fellow-students at Oxford's Lady Margaret Hall wept yesterday: "Sarah said she was very worried about not getting a first.

"She'd won a scholarship to go on to Harvard University in America, and she said she would be the only one there with a second-class degree.

"I thought she was joking."

Sarah's grieving brother David, 20, said: "The system at Oxford puts so much

TURN TO PAGE TWO

EXCLUSIVE: *The picture that will turn Gazza green*

BHOY BLUE

By ANNA SMITH

GAZZA waves a Celtic scarf with a bunch of Parkhead fans – just before bursting into a chorus of the Irish anthem.

The Rangers ace posed for our amazing photo at a boozy St Patrick's Day bash in New York – not knowing it would find its way back to Scotland.

FULL STORY ~ Page Five

PLAY THREE DAYS TO PAYDAY PAGE 22

Daily Record

Tuesday, April 22, 1997   28p

SCOTLAND'S CHAMPION

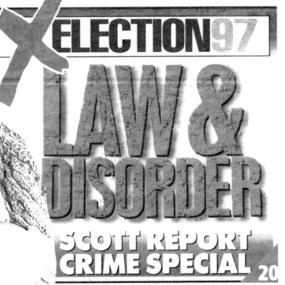

PLAY £75,000 CASH SCRATCH! PAGE 25

ELECTION 97

LAW & DISORDER

SCOTT REPORT CRIME SPECIAL 20

SNAP HAPPY

HERE'S the first picture from the love match everyone wanted to see.

Tennis ace Andre Agassi says "I do" to film star Brooke Shields at a star-studded service in Carmel, California, on Saturday.

Beautiful Brooke, 31, looked stunning in her £20,000 silk wedding gown.

And Andre, 26, looked confident and relaxed in his dinner jacket – Armani, of course.

The happy couple are now honeymooning in a secret location in the South Seas.

THAT'S RICH: *Fury as fat-cat directors cash in*

£750,000 for bosses.. and T-shirts for their workers

By COLIN CALDER

THREE bosses gave themselves nearly £750,000 in bonuses yesterday – and offered their 100 staff a T-SHIRT each.

An angry worker at Dundee-based Shield Diagnostic said: "I think most of us will tell them where to stuff it."

The fat-cats paid themselves the cash even though the firm is set to reveal a **LOSS** of £1million.

TURN TO PAGE TWO

54321 YOU COULD WIN £10,000

SEE PAGE 12 Token collect

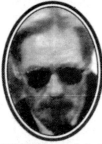

DEPORTED ... McCafferty

Get -lost, Mad Dog!

By DAVID THOMPSON

MASS killer Archie "Mad Dog" McCafferty yesterday tried to get the Daily Record to bankroll his new life in Scotland.

We sent him away with his tail between his legs.

Glasgow-born McCafferty, 49, faces being deported to Scotland this week after serving time for four savage killings in Australia.

He told ex-wife Mandy, now back with him, to sell us his story.

Mandy, 31, offered us an exclusive interview if we gave her "my ticket and a bit of spending money" to fly to Scotland.

She said we'd also have to pay McCafferty.

In a phone call from Australia, Mandy said: "Archie wants to know if you want the story.

"You'll have to talk to him about how much he wants.

"But as far as me getting over there, it would have to be my ticket and a bit of spending money and then you would have the story."

We told her we were not interested.

Mandy met McCafferty

TURN TO PAGE FIVE

SHAFTED

FROM COAL TO DOLE ... Monktonhall miners staked own cash on saving pit

Money men throw 300 miners on slag heap

MINERS who forked out to save their pit were thrown on the slag heap yesterday.

Money men pulled the plug on Monktonhall Colliery without bothering to tell 300 workers.

Devastated union rep Alex Bennett learned his job was gone when he turned on the radio.

He stormed: "It's an awful way to find out.

"We've been kept completely in the dark."

A total of 160 miners ploughed £10,000 each into saving the pit at Newton, near Edinburgh.

Waverley Mining later invested cash in return for a 49 per cent stake.

But yesterday they withdrew support.

Chief executive Willie McLucas said: "There was simply not an ongoing business there."

YOU'RE THE PITS ~ Page Two

PLUS 54321 £10,000 MUST BE WON
PAGE 16

sunday mail

55p   April 27, 1997   4131

STREET STAR'S SECRET BOOB!

DOPEY Don Brennan lost the plot totally yesterday.

Geoff Hinsliff, who plays demented Don in Coronation Street, broke all TV rules by sensationally revealing the soap's storyline.

Don – locked up in a secure hospital since driving arch-enemy

Mike Baldwin's wife Alma into a canal – is set for a chilling return to the Street.

He'll break out of hospital to haunt Baldwin – and leave all the other Street characters looking anxiously over their shoulders.

The star revealed the shocking plot to Corrie fans at a celebrity golf tournament in Scotland yesterday.

And it's sure to land him in soapy bubble with bosses, who were determined to keep their storylines secret

TURN TO PAGE 3

SCOTLAND THE GRAVE

HOPES OF A NATION 1979 ~ 1997

- INVERGORDON
- LINWOOD
- GARTCOSH
- CATERPILLAR
- SCOTT LITHGOW
- TIMEX
- BATHGATE
- RAVENSCRAIG
- ROSYTH

THEY never cared for the people of Scotland. They never cared for anyone but themselves.

But this Thursday the people of Scotland have a golden opportunity to dump this Government.

IT is a chance for a new beginning... for a new Scotland.

For 18 years, Scotland has suffered grievously at the hands of a Government that put profit before people.

For Scotland, the devastation of its industrial heritage is a litany of despair.

FOR the Tories, it is a roll of shame. On Thursday Scotland must vote for a new tomorrow and ditch the party of yesterday.

GO NOW Mr MAJOR... Pages 6 and 7

54321 YOU COULD WIN £10,000
PAGE 14

INSIDE Home RECORD
36-PAGE PROPERTY EXTRA

Baxter swap op outrage

A HEART-broken gran yesterday slammed docs who refused to carry out a life-saving liver transplant on her granddaughter.

Margaret Pirie claimed they refused to help tragic Michelle Pirie because the 15-year-old had taken Ecstasy.

But she pointed out soccer legend Jim Baxter got TWO liver transplants after ruining his health through years of boozing.

Michelle, from Aberdeen, died of liver failure in hospital – three days after being turned down for a transplant.

FULL STORY PAGE 8

Pammy in nude bust-up

BAYWATCH babe Pamela Anderson quit a multi-million pound movie because the producers wanted her to simulate sex on screen.

She denies breaking a contract which included filming nude scenes.

But Pam, 30, is being sued for £3million damages for refusing to make the film Hello, She Lied.

The star sat stony-faced in a Los Angeles court yesterday as the case began.

Pam's lawyers claimed she demanded script changes – but they were never made.

One scene had her stripping off and lathering soap on her body in a shower. She jumps into

TURN TO PAGE 3

WIDOW'S PLEA: *Let's complete his 'unfinished business'*

WIN IT FOR JOHN

LEGACY ... Lady Smith, left, urges voters to back her husband's vision

THE widow of John Smith begged the Scottish people yesterday to complete the late Labour leader's "unfinished business".

She urged them to vote Labour in a moving pre-poll message issued exclusively through the Daily Record.

Baroness Elizabeth Smith went abroad at the start of the election campaign, fearing it would be too painful.

But she also felt it was important to send her endorsement of the party – and to urge Scots to vote for a Labour victory.

She wrote: "In these last few days of this campaign, I want to say how much I urge

TURN TO PAGE TWO

MAJOR'S LAST THROW: *Pages 10 & 11* ● **BELL'S BATTLE ZONE:** *Pages 20 & 21*

Daily Record

Wednesday, April 30, 1997   28p

SCOTLAND'S CHAMPION

STREETS AHEAD!

CORRIE'S CROWNING GLORY – PAGE 3

FURIOUS ... Betty

Bungling bankers grabbed my home

EXCLUSIVE
BY STEPHEN MARTIN

BUNGLING bankers left an innocent couple in shock when they tried to repossess the WRONG HOUSE.

Workmen sent by the Clydesdale Bank broke into Betty and Bob Smith's cottage and caused hundreds of pounds worth of damage.

But the Smiths don't owe the Clydesdale a penny.

They are not even customers.

The couple came home from work to find their locks changed, their alarm system removed and their water switched off.

The repo men also sealed the toilet, letter box and CAT FLAP.

Bob, 53, smashed a kitchen

TURN TO PAGE FIVE

BETRAYED BY 18 YEARS OF TORY SHAME

BY ANNA SMITH

ELIZABETH McKEAG'S shattered life sums up the obscenity of 18 years of Tory rule.

The 71-year-old granny was crippled by a blunder in a cash-starved hospital.

Now she's trapped in a life of pain, cared for by a system stretched to the limit by savage cuts.

● **DON'T LET BETTY DOWN** ~ *Page 6* ● **CRIPPLED BY NEGLECT** ~ *Centre Pages*

Daily Record

28p

SCOTLAND'S CHAMPION

MAY 1, 1997
ELECTION SPECIAL

☑ **Tick for your future**

Tick for more misery ☑

- [ ] **NEW SCHOOLS**
- [ ] **NEW JOBS**
- [ ] **NEW NHS**
- [ ] **NEW HOPE**
- [ ] **NEW LABOUR**

- **TAX RISES** [ ]
- **SEX & SLEAZE** [ ]
- **FAT CATS** [ ]
- **DECEIT & LIES** [ ]
- **SAME OLD TORIES** [ ]

☒ **LABOUR**

TONY'S TRIUMPH ENDS 18 YEARS OF MISERY

Daily Record
28p VICTORY EDITION

LABOUR LANDSLIDE SENSATION

WIPE-OUT

Scotland boots out all ten Tories

IN SAFE HANDS ... New Prime Minister Tony Blair hugs wife Cherie last night.

THE Tories were wiped out in Scotland last night as Tony Blair swept to power in a landslide.

He romped home with an incredible majority to end 18 years of Tory hurt.

Blair, at 43, will be the youngest Prime Minister this century.

And he'll have the biggest Labour majority **EVER**.

In Scotland, all 10 Tory MPs were turfed out.

Scots Secretary Michael Forsyth was first to lose his seat.

By 3am, the rout was complete when the Tories' last hope – Foreign Secretary Malcolm Rifkind – was beaten.

In England, the biggest casualty

TURN TO PAGE 2

OUT FORSYTH

OUT LANG

OUT RIFKIND

BLAIR: I WON'T LET YOU DOWN 2&3 **WE'RE A TORY-FREE ZONE** 4&5

BURNS SACKED

Fans' fury as McCann boots out Celtic manager

BACK PAGE

Daily Record

Saturday, May 3, 1997   28p

SCOTLAND'S CHAMPION

GOOD NEWS AT TEN

MOVING PICTURE... Tony and Cherie with kids Euan, 13, Nicholas, 11, and Kathryn, nine

PRIME MINISTER Tony Blair moved his family into 10 Downing Street yesterday.

He hugged wife Cherie and their three children, and vowed: "We will rebuild the nation.

"Enough of talking. It is time to do."

Blair had led Labour to a dazzling 179-seat majority over John Major's shattered Tories.

The massacre was the worst in living memory, and left the Conservatives without a single seat in Scotland.

By TOM BROWN

Later, Blair made Scots colleague Gordon Brown his Chancellor.

Another Scot, Robin Cook, was named Foreign Secretary.

While Labour celebrated, Major was falling on his sword.

The scramble to succeed him began as soon as he announced he was stepping down. And desperate Tory pleas for unity were forgotten as the candidates jockeyed for position.

BLAIR'S NEW BRITAIN: Pages 2, 3, 4, 5, 6, 7, 8, 9, 11, 20, 21, 60 and 61

Daily Record

Monday, May 5, 1997 — 28p

SCOTLAND'S CHAMPION

PEOPLE'S PREMIER: *Britain's new leader keeps it cool and casual*

TONY'S BREATH OF FRESH BLAIR!

Labour deliver £120m Rosyth job joy

By BILLY ADAMS

NEW Defence Secretary George Robertson got right down to business yesterday.

He wasted no time in giving the go-ahead for a £120million refit to atom sub HMS Sceptre.

And it safeguarded 3200 jobs at Rosyth Royal Dockyard.

Union chief Brian Negus said: "I'm sure George had a smile on

DOWN TO BUSINESS... Liddell and Dewar

his face when he signed."

The Fife dockyard lost out in 1993 after a series of lucrative sub refits went to Devonport.

Now Rosyth is in line to refit up to three subs.

Meanwhile, Brian Wilson and Henry McLeish were yesterday vying to become Scottish Secretary Donald Dewar's right-hand man.

Wilson is tipped to take over Scottish education and social work while employment will probably go to McLeish.

And last night, MP Helen Liddell was given a top Treasury job. She said she was "stunned".

TRENDSETTER ... relaxed Tony at church yesterday

LAID-BACK Premier Tony Blair yesterday blew away the stuffed shirts as he eased into his new job.

He dumped the role's starchy image – and the swanky Jaguar – as he led the family to Sunday service in a Ford people-carrier.

Looking relaxed and

TURN TO PAGE 3 ▶

BLAIR FORCE BRITAIN
Pages 2, 3, 4, 8 and Centre Pages

Daily Record

Thursday, May 8, 1997 — 28p

SCOTLAND'S CHAMPION

9 IN A ROW

Daily Record 16-PAGE SOUVENIR SPECIAL

16 PAGES OF JOBS INSIDE

FREE COLOUR PULLOUT

Why I told all on gay shame Hirst

By KENNY FARQUHARSON

A TOP Tory yesterday admitted revealing the gay sex stories that brought down Michael Hirst.

But Arthur Bell denied he was guilty of betrayal, saying he did it for the good of the party.

The row plunged the Tories into turmoil, days after their general election wipeout.

Bell, chairman of the Scottish Tory Reform Group, hit out after Hirst broke his

SPOKE OUT... Bell

six-week silence on the affair.

In his first interview since resigning over "past indiscretion" in his private life, Hirst spoke of his bitterness that colleagues in his own party caused his downfall.

"I am very sad," he said, "that in the wake of that there is a stench surrounding the Tory party in Scotland. That's not fair."

Hirst endorsed newspaper reports accusing Bell of "spreading the poison".

And he hinted he was ousted because some colleagues didn't want him to strengthen his position at the

TURN TO PAGE TWO

NINE IN A ROAR

By JAMIE MACASKILL

RAMPANT Rangers last night roared to a record-equalling nine-in-a-row league championships.

Paul Gascoigne, Alan McLaren and Ally McCoist kicked off the celebrations as fans across the country broke out the bubbly.

The Ibrox side wrote their place in the history books with a 1-0 win over Dundee United at Tannadice.

A headed Brian Laudrup goal sent 6000 travelling fans in to ecstasy.

Early this morning, more than 2000 fans at Ibrox welcomed the team home as stars including Jorg Albertz and Charlie Miller danced on the coach roof.

Some fans even joined their heroes on the top of the bus for a victory jig.

Hundreds more converged on George Square for a title-winning party.

Rangers' ninth win equals Old Firm rivals Celtic's run in the 60s and 70s.

NINE AND DANDY
~ 60, 61, 62, 63 and 64

74

Daily Record

Saturday, May 10, 1997   28p

SCOTLAND'S CHAMPION

5 FREE GOES ON THE LOTTO
PAGE 30

8 FREE SCRATCHCARDS

£750 CASH SCR
LOTTERY SYN

CHANCE A	CHANCE B
02 03 06 08 15 36	12 18 19 36 42 47

MAY 10

Super Ally is singing the Blues

ALLY McCOIST has helped Rangers become Scotland's top team again – now he wants to be top of the pops.

Fans at Ibrox today will hear Ally sing lead vocals on a new single called Glasgow Rangers.

And the team are set to perform it on a future National Lottery show.

PAGE THREE

Bish buys into randy Rev road

DISGRACED Bishop Roddy Wright has set up home in a cosy new love-nest.

And one of his new neighbours is a married former priest who quit the Church for love.

Roddy, the former Bishop of Argyll and the Isles, is now a house-husband who stays home while lover Kathy MacPhee goes to work.

PAGE TWO

GERI'S KISS FOR 'VERY SEXY' CHARLES

BALD SPICE ... Geri shows hot-and-bothered Charles what Girl Power is all about

PRINCE'S BUST ... Geri arrives for the gala night

BOLD SPICE

By THOMAS QUINN

SPICE GIRL Geri made Prince Charles go bright red by snogging him at a posh gala last night.

She patted the prince's bum and told him: "You know, I think you're very sexy."

The rest of the group giggled as she added: "We could spice up your life."

Charles was covered in lipstick after meeting the girls, who were performing at the 21st anniversary royal gala for the Prince's Trust.

He turned down an invitation from Posh Spice

TURN TO PAGE FIVE

75

Driver killed by own Reliant Robin

By DAVID THOMPSON

DRIVER David Burns was run over and killed by his own Reliant Robin.

David, 31, was thrown from the Del Boy three-wheeler as he drove his girlfriend along a lonely road.

He ended up in front of the motor and was crushed when its front wheel ran over his chest.

David's girlfriend, who has not been named, needed treatment for minor injuries.

The accident happened on

KILLER ... Reliant Robin

the A87 near Broadford on Skye. Police, who have been investigating for 10 days, admit they are baffled by the bizarre accident.

A spokesman said: "It took place on a straight stretch of road. The car went out of control and there were no other vehicles involved."

Archie Campbell, who owns the caravan site where the couple stayed, said: "David seemed to be a motor-cycle and three-wheeler enthusiast."

A report has gone to the procurator fiscal

STRONGMAN JAILED IN £20m DRUG STING

SHAMED ... Forbes Cowan

THE world's strongest man was yesterday jailed for his part in a £20million drugs run.

Forbes Cowan and four other gang members were given a total of 44 years.

They had tried to smuggle three tons of cannabis from Africa to Scotland but were caught by an elaborate Customs sting.

By IAIN FERGUSON

Professional muscleman Cowan, 33, twice won the World's Strongest Man title.

He overpowered several police when they pounced on the gang. But the brute turned to jelly when they threatened to bring in dogs.

A police insider said: "It was hilarious. He

TURN TO PAGE SIX

Daily Record

Thursday, May 15, 1997 — 28p

SCOTLAND'S CHAMPION

TODAY

Recruitment RECORD

16 PAGES OF JOBS

OUR PLEDGE: TO MAKE IT A DEVO DOUBLE

YES! YES!

Together we'll win Scottish Parliament

BY THE EDITOR

TODAY the Daily Record makes a solemn pledge: We will fight alongside the Scottish people to win a parliament for Scotland.

In the Queen's Speech yesterday Tony Blair's government set out its plans to hold a referendum on Scottish devolution.

It will take place this autumn, probably on September 11. The government confirmed two questions will be asked:

Do you want a Scottish parliament?

Should it have power to raise its own revenue?

Until that vote, the Record will have one goal in mind – to ensure Scotland delivers

TURN TO PAGE 7

● **BRITAIN'S NEW DEAL – 6&7** ● **SCOTLAND'S NEW DEAL – 8**

Daily Record

Friday, May 16, 1997

28p

SCOTLAND'S CHAMPION

Benn cleared

BOXING idol Nigel Benn was sensationally cleared yesterday of ripping a former pal's face open with a glass ashtray.

The ex-world champ walked free after two prosecution witnesses dramatically changed their tune.

The judge saw Benn WINKING at one of them as she testified.

Several burly associates of Benn shouted: "Yes!" in the public gallery as he was acquitted.

But he faces a £100,000 damages claim from one-time friend "Rolex Ray" Sullivan, who says Benn left him a bloodied mess in a glitzy London club.

And the judge told Benn he must pay his own costs, estimated at £100,000, because he "brought the prosecution on himself".

"Dark Destroyer" Benn, 33, was accused of glassing Sullivan at Legends nightclub in Mayfair last September.

The pair were once like brothers. But the court heard they fell out

WINKING ... Benn

TURN TO PAGE TWO

DIVINELY BROWN

HUGH'S that girl looking just Cannes-tastic as she soaks up the Riviera sun? The bikini-clad stunner was left to slap on her own tan oil, even though her boyfriend wasn't far away.

It just shows you can't take anything for granted when you're getting divinely brown.

ALL IS REVEALED ON PAGE 5

RECORD INVESTIGATION

GREEDY BOSSES STITCH UP OUR JOBS

By ANNA SMITH, Chief Reporter

SCOTS textile workers were stabbed in the back by greedy bosses, the Record can reveal.

Seventy sewing machines were shipped to a Moroccan sweatshop just days before 300 jobs were axed.

Staff at Alexandra Workwear thought the company was expanding. But their jobs were replaced by £4-a-day slave labour.

FULL STORY ~ Centre Pages

sunday mail

55p   May 18, 1997   4134

Sarwar in shocker

BRIBE SCANDAL ROCKS SCOTS MP

GOVAN ELECTION STORM

ELECTION JOY...Mohammed Sarwar celebrates with wife Perveen

MILLIONAIRE MP Mohammed Sarwar was at the centre of a bung scandal last night.

Labour launched a probe into claims he paid an election rival £5,000 to run a losing campaign.

It's claimed the new MP for Glasgow Govan handed the cash – stuffed into a carrier bag – to rival Badar Islam

He reportedly told Badar: "If you feel any danger, I will pay you £100,000."

Last night sources close to Mr Sarwar claimed the whole episode was an elaborate set-

THE INSIDE STORY Pages 4,5,7 and 12

up. But the new MP is to be questioned by the Chief Whip and faces action if he has done anything improper.

Badar reportedly told friends: "Sarwar asked me to ease off my canvassing and said I would be compensated.

"After our first meeting I didn't bother canvassing for about a month."

Cash–and–carry boss Mr Sarwar, 44, held the seat for Labour with a 2,914 majority over the Scottish National Party, while Independent Labour candidate Badar polled 319 votes.

The police are already investigating vote-rigging allegations.

Daily Record

Monday, May 19, 1997   28p

SCOTLAND'S CHAMPION

PICTURE EXCLUSIVE

DUNBLANE BRIDE'S TEARS FOR MUM

PAGES 6 & 7

Cadete to sue

CRISIS club Celtic were rocked again last night when Portuguese ace Jorge Cadete threatened to sue Fergus McCann.

The star striker claims the Parkhead supremo owes him £400,000 over his transfer last year.

And he says he will never pull on the Hoops again if he doesn't get his cash.

**FULL STORY
BACK PAGE**

Di shows the strain

NEW pictures of Princess Di taken by her pal Lord Snowdon show the strain of her life alone.

The snaps, to publicise her big charity frock sell-off, are meant to portray a smiling, confident woman of the world.

Instead, she looks drained and still emotionally scarred by her split from Charles.

**FULL STORY
PAGE 12**

MP SARWAR FLIES INTO NEW STORM

MAN IN THE MIDDLE ... MP Sarwar needed a police escort at Glasgow Airport last night

LABOUR MP Mohammed Sarwar was fighting for his political life last night over claims he bribed a general election rival.

The millionaire Glasgow Govan MP threatened to sue a newspaper which accused him of paying

By JAMIE MACASKILL

Badar Islam £5000 to fight a losing campaign.

But as Sarwar flew north after being summoned to London by Labour's Chief Whip, he was rocked by explosive new allegations. His arch

TURN TO PAGE FIVE

INSIDE *Home* **RECORD**

32-PAGES OF PROPERTY

PLUS

£50,000 CASH SCRATCH
£7,000 LUCKY SEVENS   PAGE 23

Church wants mercy for pot puffers

By BILLY ADAMS

THE Kirk's General Assembly wants the police and courts to go soft on cannabis.

Church leaders backed a report yesterday saying dope-smoking is no worse than eating too much.

And they called for a Royal Commission to look at relaxing laws on the drug.

They want users kept out of court and given warnings instead.

Some Church of Scotland ministers also feel dope should be legalised for people who take it for medical reasons.

The Rev Jim Cowie, presenting the findings of a two-year study on the issue, said people guilty of cannabis possession should be given cautions and counselling instead of fines or jail.

Sinful

He claimed the drug was no more sinful than booze, fags or overeating.

The Rev Bill Wallace, the convener of the Kirk's Board of Social Responsibility, wants a full public debate on the issue.

He said: "There are a lot of groups pushing for a change in the law, and it seems to us any change should be through a Royal Commission."

Prime Minister Tony Blair slammed the Church's proposals when they were first aired in March, and is expected to oppose them again.

He is set to appoint an American style drug Tsar as part of a crackdown.

The Assembly also slammed companies who target alcopops and booze-laced sweets at children.

RECORD EXCLUSIVE

SECRET LIFE OF SCHOOLGIRL, 36
FULL AMAZING STORY – Page 18

GOVAN SLEAZE ROW: *Sarwar hits back*

£5000 WAS LOAN NOT BRIBE

SARWAR ... protested innocence

By KENNY FARQUHARSON

LABOUR MP Mohammed Sarwar has admitted to party bosses that he gave £5000 to a rival general election candidate.

But he insisted the cash he handed to Badar Islam was **NOT** a bribe, but a loan.

The millionaire Govan MP gave Islam the money to help him with his huge debts, according to Scottish Labour sources.

Sarwar was carpeted on Sunday by Labour's Chief Whip Nick Brown.

But he was adamant there was "nothing dishonest or improper" over the exchange of cash, said the source.

The explanation saved him from being suspended as a Labour MP.

Sarwar, 44, yesterday issued a writ for defamation against the Sunday paper

TURN TO PAGE SEVEN

81

Daily Record

8-PAGE CUP FINAL SPECIAL INSIDE

Saturday, May 24, 1997   28p

SCOTLAND'S CHAMPION

Ex-nun is surrogate mum of 5

A FORMER nun was a surrogate mother to five babies including twins.

Theresa McLaughlin said she was pregnant six times in six years, and miscarried twice.

Three of the children went to one couple.

Divorcee McLaughlin, 40, from Dumbarton, is now a child care worker in the north of England.

She became a nun at 18 and left the order to train as an auxiliary nurse four years later.

Last night, she said: "I do not have a problem with the ethics.

"I see it as helping people who need help. I have always liked helping

TURN TO PAGE 2

Dead end Street for Corrie stars

THREE top Coronation Street stars were axed last night.

The move came after Mavis – actress Thelma Barlow – quit the soap.

The three characters for the chop are Maureen Holdsworth, Andy McDonald and Bill Webster.

Bill Tarmey, who plays Rovers' landlord Jack Duckworth, said: "I'd be shocked if it is true."

Since the arrival of Scot Brian Park as executive producer, the axe has been hanging over many of the Street fans' favourites.

And last night, insiders said morale in the show – once the most popular in Britain – was at an all-time low.

SEE PAGE 8

KEY TO THE DOOR: *Family win our £100,000 house*

HOUSE ABOUT THAT... Robert, Andrena and son Sean

HOME FREE!

Daily Record made our dream come true

THE super-lucky Simpson family yesterday scooped their £100,000 dream home – thanks to the Daily Record.

Hard-up Andrena, Robert and two-year-old son Sean got the news just days after deciding the SAME house was too expensive.

The family decided they could never afford the Barratt showhouse just 200 yards from their present home, but last night the overjoyed threesome picked up the keys.

Andrena beamed: "It is beyond our wildest dreams."

And Robert added: "This is great news. We never thought we would win."

By ROGER HANNAH

FULL STORY ~ Pages 2 & 3

5 FREE GOES ON THE £14m ROLLOVER LOTTO

CHANCE A   12 15 24 30 42 47

CHANCE B   05 06 13 25 28 41

May 24

PAGE 28

Daily Record

Thursday, May 29, 1997   28p

SCOTLAND'S CHAMPION

Heart scare rocks Bob Dylan

By JOHN DINGWALL

MUSIC legend Bob Dylan was in hospital last night with a serious heart problem.

Dylan, 56 on Saturday, suffered severe chest pains.

Doctors diagnosed potentially-fatal histoplasmosis, which produces symptoms similiar to TB.

His planned British tour, with Van Morrison as support, was immediately cancelled. It included a date at Glasgow's SECC next Tuesday.

Dylan has also pulled out of a massive outdoor show in Cork on Sunday night in front of

PAINS... Bob Dylan

20,000 fans but Morrison will still appear.

A Dylan spokesman said: "There will need to be a period of recuperation. It is not known how long a recovery will take."

Dylan shot to fame in the folk music boom of the early 1960s and was regarded as a spokesman for his generation.

But he switched to electric rock soon after, then changed styles many times to create a series of acclaimed albums.

They sold millions and many other acts covered his songs like The Times They Are a Changin'.

Last year, he allowed the children of Dunblane to alter the lyrics to his hit song, Knockin' On Heaven's Door, to include an anti-gun message.

Blair blast over huge rises for fat-cat lotto bosses

YOUR NUMBER IS UP!

THAT'S YOUR LOTT ... Camelot bosses David Rigg, Tim Holley, David Clark and Peter Murphy have sparked outrage

By BILL CAVEN

FURIOUS Tony Blair last night blasted lotto bosses for awarding themselves huge pay rises.

He is poised to give Camelot the boot when their licence comes up for renewal.

The Prime Minister, who branded the rises "a total disgrace", is so angry he made it clear he will be carpeting Camelot chairman Sir George Russell.

A Heritage Department spokesman said: "If **TURN TO PAGE FIVE**

INSIDE: 16 PAGES OF JOBS

8 FREE SCRATCH CARDS

5 FREE GOES ON THE LOTTO

CHANCE A   CHANCE B

JUNE 7   14 34 37 40 41 47   19 20 41 42 45 48

PAGE 22

Horrids boot out 'scruffy' Scottish teachers

EXCLUSIVE
By DAVID THOMPSON

TWO teachers from one of Scotland's poshest schools were banned from snobs' shop Harrods – for wearing shorts.

Gerry Burns and Frank Morris were stopped by doormen as they tried to take a party of pupils to the store as a treat.

They were told they were breaking Harrods' strict dress code by flashing their hairy legs.

And the youngsters from St Aloysius College in Glasgow, on an outing to London, refused to go inside without them.

Hairy

A Harrods spokesman said sniffily: "Shorts, which might look good on a sprinter but not on a hairy male strutting around the store, are not acceptable in elegant surroundings.

"Tailored shorts and Bermuda shorts are perfectly acceptable.

"What we do not allow are skimpy shorts so brief they leave little to the imagination.

"We expect people to be dressed for the pleasurable experience of shopping, not for the running track. Respectability is the word."

School bursar Tom Ralph said: "I think the school would expect pupils to

TURN TO PAGE NINE

OASIS NOEL WED IN VEGAS

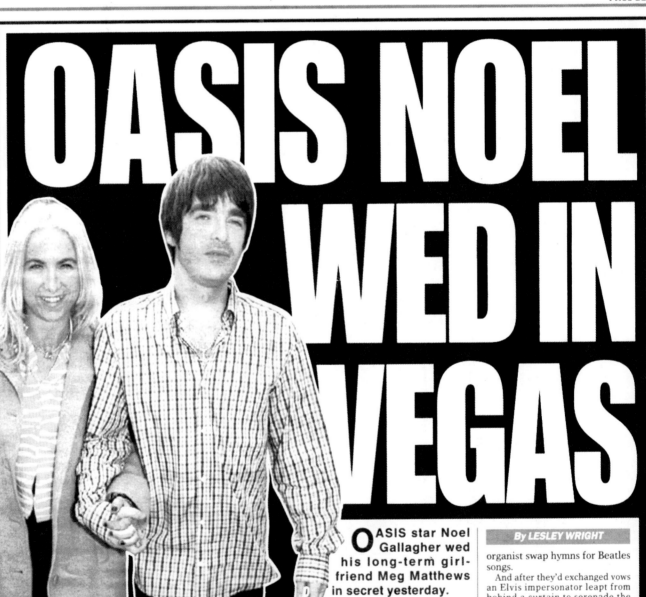

DEFINITELY MARRIED... Noel and Meg

O ASIS star Noel Gallagher wed his long-term girlfriend Meg Matthews in secret yesterday.

The couple got hitched in a £10,000 private ceremony at the Little Church of the West in Las Vegas – where Elvis Presley married Priscilla.

The Fab Four fans made the

By LESLEY WRIGHT

organist swap hymns for Beatles songs.

And after they'd exchanged vows an Elvis impersonator leapt from behind a curtain to serenade the giggling pair with Love Me Tender and Falling In Love With You.

Brother Liam and wife Patsy Kensit, who wed in secret earlier this year, were missing.

But Noel's mum Peggy and Meg's

TURN TO PAGE FIVE

---

the PUNTER 8-PAGE DERBY SPECIAL INSIDE

2 FREE GOES ON THE MIDWEEK LOTTO

JUNE 11

CHANCE A
.05 12 18 38 41 48

CHANCE B
07 25 30 37 39 45

PAGE 27

Daily Record

Wednesday, June 11, 1997   28p

SCOTLAND'S CHAMPION

HOLS FOR 2
IN GRAN CANARY TO BE WON! (PAGE 31)

CASH SCARE OVER GIANT CONCERTS

£1m ROCK TICKET PROBE

AT RISK ... fans may miss superstar Diana Ross

BOSS ... Judy Clancy

By DAVID THOMPSON

SCOTLAND'S top rock ticket agency was at the centre of a £1million probe last night.

It's feared thousands of fans who have bought tickets through TOCTA could lose out.

But frantic promoters are desperately trying to play down fears that huge concerts like T in the Park, Wet Wet Wet, U2, Diana Ross and Primal Scream could be hit.

TOCTA – The Official Concert Ticket Agency – called in a leading firm of insolvency experts after days of speculation about its future.

The firm, run by businesswoman Judy Clancy, acts as a middleman between fans and concert promoters.

Ticket outlets, which deal with millions of pounds of fans' cash, closed for business on Monday.

Last night music industry insiders were stunned that a business like TOCTA could have run into trouble.

One said: "TOCTA were in a no-lose

TURN TO PAGE TWO

MOVING ON ... Tommy

Burns for Reading

DUMPED Celtic boss Tommy Burns will today become the new manager of Reading.

Burns met John Madejski – the millionaire chairman of the English First Division side – last week.

And despite offers from clubs north and south of the border, Burns has opted for the Elm Park outfit.

FULL STORY - BACK PAGE

FAVOURITE ... Hague

Hague is odds on

WILLIAM Hague was last night installed as odds-on favourite to be the next Tory leader – despite losing the first round vote to Ken Clarke.

Former Chancellor Clarke scored 49 votes to ex-Welsh Secretary Hague's 41.

Michael Howard and Peter Lilley pulled out of the

TURN TO PAGE TWO

Daily Record

Thursday, June 12, 1997   28p

SCOTLAND'S CHAMPION

2 TOYOTA CELICAS TO BE WON!

YOUR PERSONAL NUMBER

.2673676

PAGE 54

Ice War Joe is a love cheat

EXCLUSIVE
By ANNA SMITH

ICE Cream Wars convict Joe Steele was branded a rat by his jilted lover last night.

Carla Wilson said Steele wrote her a string of steamy letters from his prison cell.

She spent years trekking across Scotland to visit him.

And when Steele was released, the lovebirds spent an idyllic three days at a hotel hideaway. But

SPLIT ... Carla and Steele

he dumped her the next week.

Last night, Carla sobbed: "His plan was that we would go away together, set up home and have babies.

"I stood by him for three years. Now I've just been dumped."

Carla, 35, added: "It's as if the old Joe has been left in prison and this is somebody I don't recognise."

The romance started after she watched a TV programme questioning his conviction – and she wrote to him.

Steele is to wed childhood sweetheart Dolly Brannan next month.

Quizzed about the letters to Carla, he said: "I was serving a long sentence. I had to do something to keep me going."

FULL STORY – Pages 4 & 5

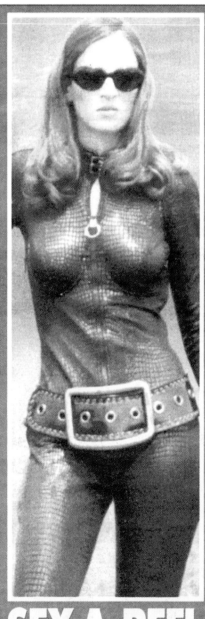

SEX A-PEEL
Uma's sexy Avengers gear

PICTURE EXCLUSIVE – PAGE THREE

VICTORY: *Blair wins total ban on pistols*

DAY OF THE GUN IS OVER

By BRENDAN MURPHY

TONY BLAIR lived up to his word last night and delivered a total ban on handguns.

His pledge to the country was rammed through the Commons with an overwhelming majority of 384 to 181 in favour of banning every legally-held pistol in the UK.

And the parents of the Dunblane victims were overjoyed by the vote.

Les Morton and John Crozier – whose daughters were both murdered by crazed Thomas Hamilton – said: "We have a Tory-free Scotland and soon we will have a gun-free UK."

The Bill will almost certainly become law by August.

The only Scots MPs to vote against a total ban were Lib Dems Bob Maclennan, Malcolm Bruce and Robert Smith.

Tony Blair said: "We did this because we have a moral responsibility to the victims of Dunblane."

VICTORY – Page Two

Daily Record

Friday, June 13, 1997   28p

SCOTLAND'S CHAMPION

Nurses forced to BUY water

EXCLUSIVE
By TOM LITTLE

THIRSTY nurses have been told to pay for WATER by penny-pinching canteen chiefs.

Angels at the Victoria Infirmary in Glasgow were ordered to fork out 3p a time for a tiny mouthful of water – to cover the cost of paper cups to put it in.

The water used to be free to all staff.

But the charges were brought in after the hospital's catering contract was handed to food giants Gardner Merchant.

One angry nurse revealed: "They said it was costing too much to supply free water because of the price of paper cups.

"It is ridiculous and will be unbearable if the warm weather comes back. The only way to

TURN TO PAGE FOUR

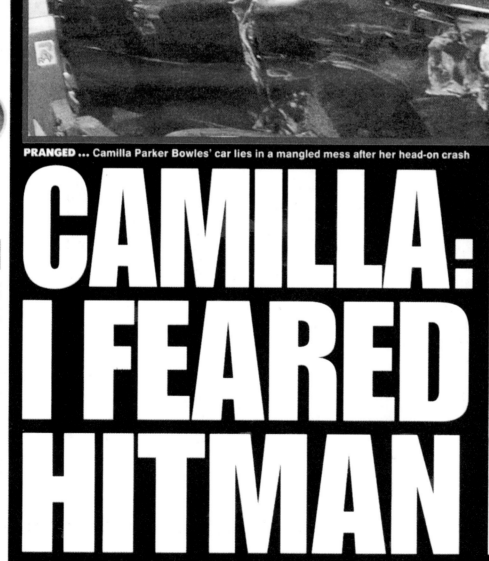

PRANGED ... Camilla Parker Bowles' car lies in a mangled mess after her head-on crash

CAMILLA: I FEARED HITMAN

SHE RAN OFF AND LEFT ME TRAPPED ~ Pages 4 and 5

By JAMES WHITAKER

CAMILLA Parker Bowles yesterday claimed she fled from a car crash fearing it was an assassination attempt.

Prince Charles' mistress told him she thought terrorists had staged the smash.

She insisted: "I panicked out of sheer terror.

"I have constantly been warned that one day I might be attacked. I thought that this is what might have happened."

She denied "scarpering" after the head-on crash without checking on the other driver, interior designer Carolyn Melville-Smith.

Camilla said that she was acting as

TURN TO PAGE FIVE

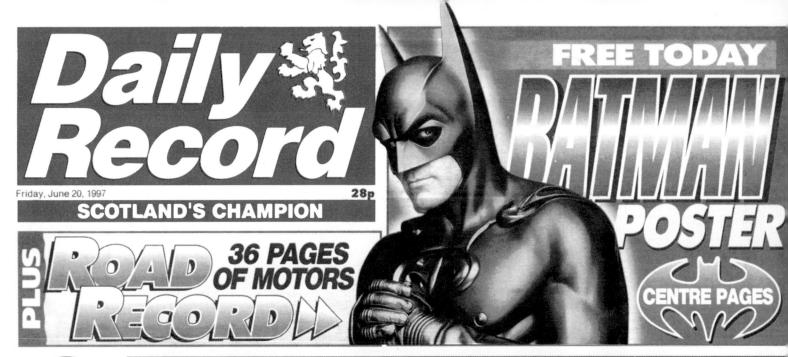

Daily Record

Friday, June 20, 1997 — 28p

SCOTLAND'S CHAMPION

PLUS ROAD RECORD — 36 PAGES OF MOTORS

FREE TODAY BATMAN POSTER — CENTRE PAGES

BOY BLUE ... Hague

MAGGIE BAGS IT FOR HAGUE

By BRENDAN MURPHY

TORY Boy William Hague was crowned Conservative leader last night after Mrs Thatcher struck from the grave.

The Iron Lady's backing delivered right-wing votes to smash old foe Ken Clarke.

One swing of her handbag destroyed Clarke's shotgun marriage with former rival John Redwood.

Hague – dubbed Hague the Vague for his woolly thinking – stormed home by 92 votes to 70.

At 36, he is the youngest Tory leader for more than 200 years.

Hague loathes Labour's plans for a Scottish Parliament and is fiercely opposed to closer links with Brussels.

Last night, ex-Chancellor Clarke and a string of heavyweights including Michael Heseltine ruled out joining his Shadow Cabinet.

HAGUE THE VAGUE Pages 6 and 7

EXCLUSIVE: *Mum's anguish as Ecstasy victim, 13, dies*

I kept my hand on Andrew's heart until it stopped beating..

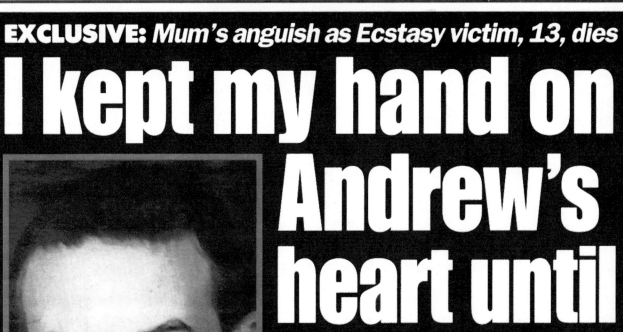

THE anguished mum of Ecstasy teenager Andrew Woodlock told yesterday how he lost his fight for life.

Distraught Phyllis revealed: "I held him and put my hand on his heart until it stopped beating."

Doctors switched off the 13-year-

By ANNA SMITH

old's life support machine after his parents were told he was brain dead.

Phyllis, 34, said: "We had to let him go. The Andrew we all knew and loved wasn't there any more. He was only

TURN TO PAGE THREE

Tomorrow WIN £5000 WITH 3 DAYS TO *PAYDAY!*

Daily Record

Saturday, June 21, 1997   28p

SCOTLAND'S CHAMPION

INSIDE

8 FREE SCRATCH CARDS

Jail visits lead to secret wedding

RECORD EXCLUSIVE

ROGUE PRIEST WEDS NUN

By ANNA SMITH, Chief Reporter

A DISGRACED ex-priest married a former nun yesterday in a hush-hush Catholic church ceremony.

Francis O'Donnell met his new wife while he was in jail for stealing rare coins and books.

Frances Dunnigan used to visit

TURN TO PAGE THREE

BRIDE AND GROOM ... O'Donnell and ex-nun Dunnigan yesterday

PICTURE: ALAN PEEBLES

Guilty Kray's hitman contract on cops

By JEFF EDWARDS

CHARLIE KRAY put out a contract on the undercover cops who condemned him to die in jail.

Kray, 70, was convicted yesterday of masterminding a £78million drugs plot that would have flooded Britain with cocaine.

He was nailed by three detectives who posed as big-time drug dealers.

Kray and the cops

Mr BIG ... Charlie

partied together as they plotted the drugs coup, Woolwich Crown Court heard.

Kray, brother of notorious gangster twins Reggie and Ronnie, knew he would almost certainly die in jail if he was convicted.

He offered gangland hitmen £100,000 to kill the three Geordie policemen.

He told a pal: "What can I lose? If I don't get a result, any sentence is a life sentence at my age."

CHARLIE TO DIE IN PRISON
Pages 6 and 7

FREE INSIDE

Essential health guide that could save your life!

Billion pound car plant joy for Scots

KOREAN car bosses are moving into top gear with plans for a billion-pound car plant for Scotland.

The scheme by Hyundai, to turn out 2,500 vehicles a week, would result in thousands of jobs.

But the planned site, on the outskirts of Glasgow, will have to fight off bids from Sunderland Bristol, and Darlington.

Insiders say Scotland could be favourite because of its road and rail infrastructure.

FULL STORY PAGE 9

Why I gave up politics to be sexy dancer to the stars

— Pages 40 and 41

He lied to his wife, family and party ... now he's to become

LORD SLEAZE

DISGRACED Tory Michael Hirst is to be sent to the Lords as a "reward" from John Major.

The peerage for wife-cheating Hirst will further tarnish Britain's tawdry honours system ...

And provide a fitting finale to Major's sleaze-ridden Government.

Major will make Hirst a peer "for political services" in his resignation honours list, to be published next month.

The move is certain to spark a storm of protest. The *Sunday*

Mail first revealed more than two months ago that Hirst had admitted a homosexual affair with party worker Paul Martin.

Hirst resigned as chairman of the Tory Party in Scotland and claimed that our story had come out because he had been the victim of a 'stitch-up' by party enemies.

In his letter of resignation to Major, Hirst cited "past indiscretion in my private life".

He said he wouldn't allow "a personal deficiency" to damage the Scottish party's election chances. And he ended:

Turn to Page 4

SHAMED ... Sir Michael Hirst

CELTIC SIGNING SENSATION
Pages 78, 79 & 80

90

Daily Record

Monday, June 23, 1997   FIRST   28p

SCOTLAND'S CHAMPION

RECORD EXCLUSIVE

COMFORT... Paul, Janet and Phyllis, centre, share memories of Andrew, top, and Leah

Picture: ALAN PEEBLES

OUR GRIEF WILL BEAT DRUGS

THE mum of boy Ecstasy victim Andrew Woodlock got a loving hug yesterday from a couple who know her agony.

Paul and Janet Betts, who lost daughter Leah

By ANNA SMITH

to the drug in 1995, travelled to Lanarkshire to comfort 13-year-old Andrew's mum Phyllis.

Both families vowed their grief will spur them on to fight the drugs menace.

UNITED BY PAIN AND ANGER ~ Pages 16, 17 RECORD VIEW ~ Page 8

SCOTS COUPLE BUY DI FROCK

Daily Record

Friday, June 27, 1997   28p

SCOTLAND'S CHAMPION

£39,000 for this little black number
PAGES 4&5

SPEECH ... Hague

Hague pleads for end to Tory civil war

By KENNY FARQUHARSON

TORY leader William Hague was last night desperately trying to stop his Scots troops tearing themselves apart.

Bitter in-fighting erupted yesterday at the Scots Tories' conference in Perth

Right-wingers attacked moderates, claiming a "left-wing militant tendency" was wrecking the party.

At the conference tonight, Hague will try to paper over the cracks in his first major speech as leader.

He will claim: "The days of disunity, factions, wings within groups, parties within parties are over.

"*It is finished. And as long as I am leader it will never come back.*"

But left-wingers are accused of plotting a Scots Tory breakaway from the UK party.

Senior right-winger Lloyd Beat hit out yesterday: "Labour had to solve its Militant problem. The Scottish Conservative Party must now do the same."

FULL STORY
Page Nine

REVVING IT UP!

FALSE PROFIT... Bunce lives it up at party

Crooked cleric's life of luxury on nicked £44,000

A CROOKED church-man took £44,000 from the pockets of the jobless and spent it on high living.

The Very Reverend Dr Michael Bunce, 47, stole the cash from a job-training scheme he ran in Brechin,

By BRIAN McCARTNEY

Angus. He squandered it on flash cars, antiques and even **FLYING LESSONS**.

Bunce smiled in the dock yesterday as he was found guilty of embezzlement. He will be sentenced later.

FULL STORY ~ Page 2 & 3

COLLARED...as Rev

TOMORROW / **8 FREE SCRATCHCARDS** / **5 GOES ON THE LOTTO**

sunday mail

55p · June 29, 1997 · 4140

Braveheart girl bears her soul in XS

Cindy's porn shocker Page 5

KING COKE

exposes Britain's biggest drugs dealer

EXCLUSIVE

TODAY we expose Britain's most evil drugs dealer.

Our amazing dossier reveals Scot Brian Doran as the mastermind in a sinister £65 million international drug smuggling syndicate.

For the first time – in amazing detail – we chart Doran's tracks from the Colombian drugs capital of the world, through millionaires' playgrounds and into Scotland.

Ex-travel agent Doran, who has previously been jailed for drug dealing, was on the verge of netting millions from his wages of sin.

But now the 52-year-old father of six faces the prospect of spending the rest of his life behind bars.

THE AMAZING STORY
Pages 2, 3, 40 and 41

Daily Record

Monday, June 30, 1997   28p

SCOTLAND'S CHAMP

FREE CAR AIR FRESHENER Page 27

SEXERCISE WITH MR M
Pages 22,23

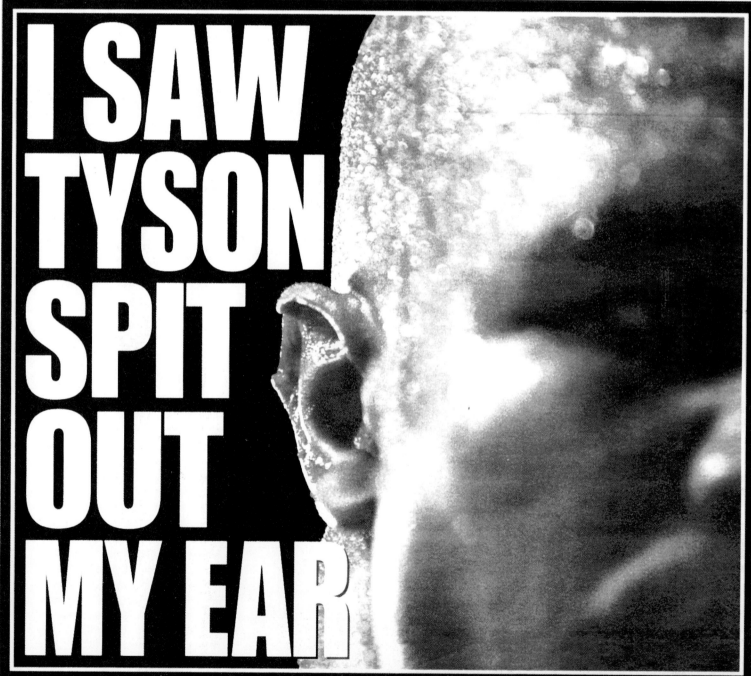

I SAW TYSON SPIT OUT MY EAR

● MIKE Tyson was branded an animal last night for his sickening ear-biting attack on Evander Holyfield. He spat the torn flesh on to the canvas. Holyfield said: "I thought he'd bitten it off completely." **SEE PAGES 2 AND 3**

Daily Record

Thursday, July 3, 1997   28p

SCOTLAND'S CHAMPION

TIGER TIM!

THE CHAMPIONSHIPS WIMBLEDON

Back page

THE BUDGET...97....THE BUDGET...97....THE BUDGET

THE

BROWN JEWELS

Schools get billions from tax on the fat cats

NHS will pick up a huge injection of cash

And there is still £3.5bn left for new jobs

BUDGET SPECIAL ~ Pages 2, 3, 4, 5, 6 and 7

Jimmy Stewart dies of heart attack

FILM legend Jimmy Stewart died yesterday at the age of 89.

The star of classics including It's A Wonderful Life suffered a heart attack at his home in Beverly Hills.

Stewart, who won an Oscar in 1940 for The Philadelphia Story, never recovered from the loss of wife Gloria.

She died in his arms from lung cancer three years ago.

The couple had been together for more than 45 years and war hero Stewart became a virtual

STEWART ... never got over wife's death

recluse after her death.

He hardly ate and took little exercise, apart from visits to the cemetery where she was buried.

Stewart, who also starred in The Glenn Miller Story, Mr Smith Goes To Washington, and Vertigo, said at the time of her death: "I don't know how I'm going to live without her.

"The only consolation is that we will soon be reunited again. Our love will continue in Heaven."

The actor with the slow drawl was almost always cast as the ordinary bloke with a heart of gold.

Stewart was rarely thought of as a romantic hero but Kim Novak, his co-star in a string of films, said: "He was the sexiest man who played opposite me in 30 years."

A WONDERFUL LIFE ~ Page 25

sunday mail

55p | *July 6, 1997* | 4141

FREE

Pages that made history ... a historic offer **Page 10**

£44,000 THEFT VICAR IS A LOVE CHEAT TOO

HE'S THE REV RAT!

BUNCE ... awaiting sentence

PARSONS ... a secret affair

EXCLUSIVE

CROOKED churchman Michael Bunce is a love cheat.

After his sins of theft and lying were exposed, we can reveal he also cheated on his wife.

Bunce, who faces jail after conviction for a £44,000 theft, had a secret affair with his secretary, Maureen Parsons.

He used secret signs to summon her after Sunday service and even used his marital bed in the rectory when his wife was out.

Maureen, 42, said: "He used and abused me. I feel such a fool."

FULL STORY – PAGE 9

ULSTER ON THE BRINK – SPECIAL REPORT: PAGES 4 AND 5

Home RECORD
28 PAGES OF PROPERTY

OH, NO!

ELVIS DEAD

OUT shoots out Tories

FREE
FRONT PAGE CLASSICS
PAGE 27

Token collect plus 55p postage

---

2 boys die as blaze guts home

by *ALLISON McLAUGHLIN*

TWO little boys were killed yesterday as fire ripped through their home.

Scott Risk died on his fifth birthday with his two-year-old brother Adam after they were trapped in a bedroom.

And last night their three-year-old brother Mark was fighting for his life in hospital.

Their devastated parents Scott, 31, and Susan, 24, survived the blaze after leaping from a window at their home in Greengairs, Lanarkshire.

The boys were pulled out by firefighters after frantic attempts by neighbours to reach them.

Screaming

Last night it was revealed that one of them, Tony Chambers, 28, had moved to the area a month ago after rescuing three boys from a house fire in England.

He said: "I can't believe this has happened to me again.

"When I saw those wee boys lying on the pavement this morning it brought it all back.

"It was so horrific the first time but at least I was able to help other neighbours get those boys out."

Tony said he was alerted to yesterday's fire by the sound of the boys' mother screaming but he was beaten

TURN TO PAGE TWO

DOLPHIN TAUGHT

Little Christopher Gowans, 4, uttered his first words while swimming with dolphins in Florida. He giggled: "I want dance..."

MY SON TO TALK

EXCLUSIVE: *Miracle that cured Christopher – Pages 2 and 3*

Daily Record

Saturday, July 12, 1997   28p

SCOTLAND'S CHAMPION

Girl cop gunned down in Ulster terror

By STEPHEN MARTIN

THREE soldiers and two RUC officers were injured when gunmen opened fire on a security patrol in Belfast last night.

Four terrorists drove up in Ford Sierra and two of them jumped out and fired about 20 shots.

Witnesses said a third man then hurled a blast bomb at the security team.

The casualties – including a policewoman – were all taken to hospital with leg injuries.

None of them was thought to be seriously hurt.

Marches

They had been patrolling an area between Loyalist and Republican strongholds on the eve of the traditional July 12 marches by the Orange Order.

A witness said: "They were just doing a vehicle check when this other car went through.

"It turned round and the gunmen got out on the other side of the patrol."

After the attack in the Ardoyne area of the city, the Sierra sped off into the Republican district.

Ulster Unionist MP Cecil Walker said: "It's diabolical when the security forces who are trying to help both communities are attacked in

TURN TO PAGE TWO

I'M PREGNANT: *Wife stuns Paul as he picks up MBE*

YOU'RE GONG TO HAVE A BABY!

SOCCER hero Paul McStay was given a gong from the Queen – and left gobsmacked by his missus yesterday.

As he showed off his MBE, wife Anne Marie announced in front of everyone: "You're going to be a dad again."

Paul was struck dumb for a full minute before hugging and kissing the mum-to-be.

He beamed: "Surprise is not the word – it's fantastic news."

Paul and Anne Marie were at Holyrood Palace in Edinburgh

TURN TO PAGE FIVE

EXPECTING... Anne Marie and Paul, left, with son Chris

SALUTE TO DUNBLANE HEROES *Page Five*

NOEL IN HIDING

By BRIAN McCARTNEY

GRIEF-STRICKEN Noel Edmonds last night went into hiding after the Glamis helicopter tragedy.

The TV star was devastated by the death of Gary Malley, nine, when a chopper crashed during a charity flight. He's vowed to meet the shattered families of Gary and other kids involved.

Last night Noel's

PR man said: "Noel is extremely upset. He has shut up shop and is staying at home to try and get things together.

"He has a very busy diary and and absolutely everything has been cancelled."

Earlier, Noel said: "I remain heartbroken that a day which **TURN TO PAGE 11**

PAL SAW COPTER CRUSH GARY ~ Page 11

Coke king jailed for 25 years

By CHARLES BEATON

THE Scot who masterminded a £65million drug smuggling operation was caged for 25 years yesterday.

Brian Doran, a former altar boy, was busted after customs swooped on a boat loaded with cocaine.

It marked the end of a three-year undercover operation which took

EVIL ... Brian Doran

customs officers to three continents.

And it smashed the evil empire which Doran ran with his Scots henchman, 43-year-old Kenneth Togher. Togher was also jailed for 25 years – and both men will have to spend another 10 years behind bars unless they each hand over more than £2million of their profits.

They were tracked down after customs men followed a trail which led from the drug cartels of Colombia right back to the junkie dens of Scotland.

In all 44 people were arrested and there were court cases in the UK, France and Spain.

Doran, 52, showed no emotion as he stood in the dock to be sentenced

TURN TO PAGE FIVE

Harry and Wills fear for mum

DIANA: I MAY QUIT BRITAIN

ON THE SPOT ... Di reveals she may leave Britain as she soaks up the sun yesterday

PRINCESS Di yesterday dropped the bombshell that she may quit Britain for good.

She said sons Wills and Harry had pleaded with her to move abroad for the sake of her sanity.

Di's dramatic revelation came as she soaked up the sun in a leopard-print swimsuit while on holiday at the French summer playground of St Tropez.

FULL STORY ~ Pages Two and Three

YEAR OF THE SPICE Centre pages / **28-PAGE Home RECORD**

99

Daily Record

Wednesday, July 16, 1997　　28p

SCOTLAND'S CHAMPION

FREE 16-PAGE OPEN SPECIAL

Assassin's curse as he guns down designer

VERSACE MURDER LINK TO MAFIA

By MARK DOWDNEY

FASHION guru Gianni Versace was shot in the head at point blank range by a hired assassin yesterday.

The gunman shouted out a curse in Italian as he pumped two bullets into the top designer.

The 50-year-old gay millionaire slumped dying at the gates of his Miami mansion.

The FBI believe Versace may have been executed over a Mafia deal that went wrong.

FASHION VICTIM... slain designer Gianni

REVENGE ~ Pages 2 and 3　　MIDAS TOUCH ~ Pages 10 and 11

Daily Record

Tuesday, July 22, 1997   28p
SCOTLAND'S CHAMPION

GORAM FACES BOOT

Back Page

PICTURE EXCLUSIVE
WHY I STRIPED FOR TIGER

Full story and pictures

Pages 16/17

DIANA HUGS CAMILA

Page 3

SOCCER KIDS, 9 FACE DRUG TESTS

SHOCKED... Johnstone   EXTREME ... Gemmell

EXCLUSIVE
By ALLISON McLAUGHLIN

SOCCER kids as young as nine are to be given random drug tests.

The crackdown is a bid to stop budding young stars being tempted by drugs.

And last night, Scotland's footballing heroes blasted the move.

Telly pundit and ex-Rangers star Derek Johnstone said: "It's absolutely ridiculous – nine is far too young."

And former Celtic great Tommy Gemmell said: "Kids that age probably don't even know

TURN TO PAGE SEVEN

INSIDE *Home* RECORD 28 PAGES OF PROPERTY

Daily Record

Wednesday, July 23, 1997   28p

SCOTLAND'S CHAMPION

Crowd's fury at police delay in hunt for Scott

By STEVE MARTIN

PARENTS last night staged a demo outside the home of the man accused of killing Scott Simpson.

Police stood guard as around 80 of them marched on Steven Leisk's flat in Aberdeen.

They were angry about the way police handled the hunt for Scott, whose body was found early yesterday.

The demonstration, in

KILLED ... Scott

Bedford Road, lasted for about half an hour before the group moved off.

Many of them walked the half-mile to the spot where Scott's body was found to add floral tributes to the dozens already in place.

Demo organiser Thomas Whyte, 23, a student at Aberdeen University, said: "This is a peaceful protest about how long it took the police to find Scott.

"People believe the search wasn't carried out properly.

"But we are all grieving for his family and the last thing anybody wants is for there to be any trouble."

HEARTBROKEN ... Princess Di comforts Elton John at the memorial service for fashion king Versace

DI'S GENTLE TOUCH FOR WEEPING ELTON

WRAPPED IN BLACK FOR VERSACE: *Pages 2&3* ● **GOODBYE GODFATHER:** *Centre Pages*

FULL STORY Pages 4 and 5

102

Daily Record

Friday, July 25, 1997

28p

SCOTLAND'S CHAMPION

DEVO DAY SPECIAL

YES! YES!

IT'S ALL YOURS... Tony Blair gives the thumbs-up to plans for a power-to-the-people Scottish Parliament yesterday

Tony's thumbs-up for new Scotland

POWER OF SCOTLAND: *Pages 2 & 3* ● **DATE WITH DESTINY:** *Pages 4 & 5*

PLUS 8-PAGE DEVO SUPPLEMENT INSIDE

103

Daily Record

Tuesday, July 29, 1997   EIRE 45p   28p

SCOTLAND'S CHAMPION

Celtic Boys' pair are held by police

EXCLUSIVE
By ANNA SMITH

TWO former officials of Celtic Boys' Club at the centre of sex abuse allegations were in custody last night.

Jim Torbett, 50, and Frank Cairney, 62, were arrested by police yesterday.

They are due to appear at Glasgow Sheriff Court today.

The move comes 10 months after the Record reported an alleged sex abuse scandal spanning more than 20 years at the club.

Torbett was a founder member of Celtic Boys' Club and resigned during Jock Stein's reign as Celtic manager.

Resigned

But he later returned in an administrative role at the club for young hopefuls.

Cairney resigned as general manager of the boys' club five years ago after a trip to America.

Last October, Torbett, of Beaconsfield Road, Kelvinside, Glasgow, and Cairney of Viewpark, Uddingston, Lanarkshire, faced charges of sexual assault and abuse of young boys when they were interviewed by detectives at Glasgow's London Road police station.

Strathclyde Police said last night: "We can confirm that two men, aged 62 and 50, have been arrested and are in police custody.

"We can confirm that the men are James Torbett and Frank Cairney."

TRAGIC END: *Gossips pushed McMaster over the edge*

LIES THAT DROVE MP TO SUICIDE

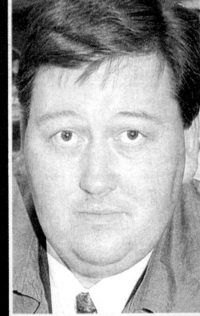

DEPRESSED ... McMaster took own life

By JAMIE MACASKILL

SCOTS MP Gordon McMaster killed himself after a desperate fight against a horror illness – and a vicious smear campaign.

The 20-stone gentle giant took his own life after a two-year battle against a condition caused by exposure to chemicals.

The flu-like symptoms – similar to Gulf War Syndrome – left the 37-year-old MP for Paisley South exhausted

TURN TO PAGE THREE

104

Daily Record

Wednesday, July 30, 1997   28p

SCOTLAND'S CHAMPION

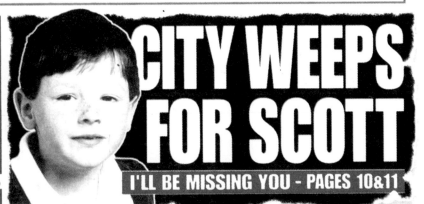

CITY WEEPS FOR SCOTT

I'LL BE MISSING YOU - PAGES 10&11

TRACIE: THE LAST CHILLING INTERVIEW

I KNEW I'D BE FOUND GUILTY

LEE HARVEY

ROAD RAGE KILLER

SCHEMING murderess Tracie Andrews knew she was going to jail BEFORE a jury convicted her of butchering her fiance.

But as she waited for yesterday's guilty verdict, she was still sticking to her story that

By ROD CHAYTOR

Lee Harvey was killed by a mystery road rage attacker.

Moments before the jury returned to Birmingham Crown Court, Andrews told me: "I know they'll find me guilty, but I didn't commit

TURN TO PAGE TWO

CAGED FOR LIFE... road rage killer Tracie Andrews outside court yesterday

● **SHE FROZE MY BLOOD ~ Pages 2&3**   ● **BAT OUT OF HELL ~ Pages 4&5**

sunday mail

55p   August 3, 1997   4145

CABINET SHOCKER

COOK AND HIS SECRET LOVER

Paolo quits Celtic

THE long-running soap opera involving Paolo di Canio and Celtic has ended. The deal is done for the Italian to move.

– BACK PAGE

Kirsty heals split

SCOTS supermodel Kirsty Hume has persuaded her future father-in-law to end a 20-year feud with her fiancé.

– PAGE 5

Yes.. I'm leaving my wife

FOREIGN Secretary Robin Cook has left his wife Margaret... after confessing to an affair with his Commons secretary.

Robin, 51, the MP for Livingston, is setting up home with 41-year-old Gaynor Regan – and has announced he takes FULL BLAME for the marriage bust-up.

Prime Minister Tony Blair last night said he was "very sorry" about the news of the break-up.

WIFE... Margaret

FULL STORY – Pages 2 and 3

106

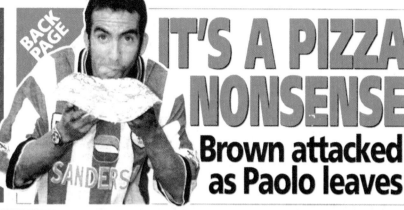

IT'S A PIZZA NONSENSE

Brown attacked as Paolo leaves

Daily Record

Thursday, August 7, 1997   28p

SCOTLAND'S CHAMPION

THE LOOK OF LOVE

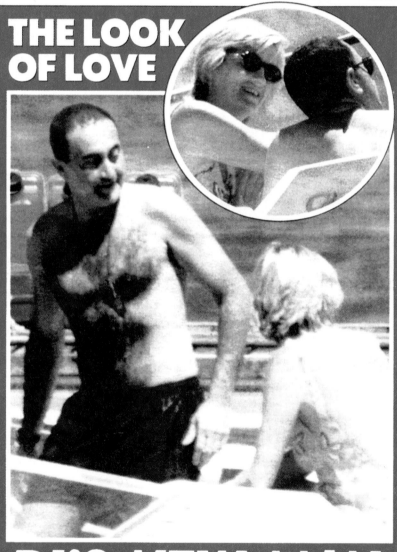

DI'S NEW MAN

PRINCESS Diana has found love again – with Harrods heir Dodi Al Fayed.

Diana, 36, slipped back into Britain yesterday morning after a secret holiday with the dashing son of tycoon Mohammed Al Fayed.

The couple had flown out together on Mohammed's private jet last Thursday, and boarded his luxury cruiser in the south of France.

Diana and Dodi, 41, spent six romantic days on the boat in Corsica, but their cover was blown when they were spotted by the paparazzi.

An informed source said: "This could be true love. They are both lovely people."

MORE AMAZING PICTURES ~ Pages 2 and 3

GUNMAN: *Cops hunt masked killer*

BOY, FIVE SHOT DEAD SAVING HIS DAD

By PAUL BYRNE

A LITTLE boy was shot dead yesterday as he tried to save his stepdad from a ruthless killer.

The gunman, wearing a motorcycle helmet, shot five-year-old Dylan Hull twice in the head.

Last night, stepdad John Bates, 28, was being treated for serious injuries to the stomach.

Neighbours heard three shots followed by John's screams.

Mary Cooper, 59, told how Dylan died in the street shortly after she reached him.

She said: "The stepfather

TURN TO PAGE NINE

Daily Record

Saturday, August 9, 1997 · 28p

SCOTLAND'S CHAMPION

8 INSIDE FREE SCRATCH CARDS

£1000 OF COOL KIDS' CLOBBER

pages 12,13

TO BE WON

Charles' amazing message to Diana

RADIANT ... Di in Bosnia yesterday

GOOD LUCK WITH DODI

By JAMES WHITAKER

PRINCE Charles has given his blessing to Diana's romance with Dodi Al Fayed.

He has told friends that he wishes his ex-wife "every happiness".

And he added: "Good luck to them."

As Diana flew into Bosnia on her anti-landmine crusade yesterday, a senior royal source said the prince enjoyed "a wry smile" when he heard about Di and Dodi.

The source added: "Whatever difficulties they may have had over the years,

TURN TO PAGE TWO

HAPPY ... Charles gave blessing to Dodi and Di

108

sunday mail

55p | August 10, 1997 | 4146

THE KISS
..that says yes, we're so in love

THIS is the kiss that lets the world know how much they're in love... Princess Diana and millionaire playboy Dodi Al Fayed are locked in an intimate embrace on board a speed boat in the Mediterranean during their holiday together in the sun.

Diana and Dodi's moment of passion is their way of declaring: "We're lovers and we don't care who knows it." And no-one can doubt it after seeing this exclusive picture.

THEIR LIPS TOUCH... and Di melts into the arms of her playboy lover Dodi Al Fayed

● Princes call him Uncle Dodi~Pages 2 & 3   ● Marriage would be disastrous~Pages 4 & 5

109

5 Ford ESCORTS TO BE WON PAGE 16 *'0898 entry*

edinburg

Well ... it's one way to look at it! (But there's loads more inside)

estival 1997

FREE INSIDE 28-PAGE FESTIVAL GUIDE

Three die in road horror

By STEVE MARTIN

A TAXI driver and two passengers died in a head-on crash last night.

Three other people were injured and rushed to hospital.

The two-car smash happened at 7.30pm outside Erskine, Renfrewshire, on the A726 road to Bishopton.

Rescuers had to cut the dead men free from the wreckage of the Ford Granada cab.

Two other passengers in the taxi, a man and a woman, were last night fighting for life at Paisley's Royal Alexandra Hospital, where they were said to be critical.

Police said a Vauxhall Vectra had been travelling downhill towards Erskine when it ploughed into the taxi which was coming uphill.

Trapped

The Vectra's driver, thought to be Norwegian, suffered serious injuries.

Meanwhile, a four-car pile-up near Edinburgh left seven people injured, including three children.

The crash happened at Carberry, near Musselburgh.

Ambulances ferried the children to Edinburgh's Sick Kids' Hospital and four adults were taken to the city's Royal Infirmary.

None of the injuries was life-threatening.

On Saturday, 26-year-old George Hannah, of Pinkston Drive, Sighthill, Glasgow, died when his car hit a barrier on the M77 at Newton Mearns, Renfrewshire.

His girlfriend, Michelle Sexton and their five-year-old son, George, were rushed to hospital but she discharged herself yesterday.

SYMBOL OF HOPE: *Princess moved by blast victim's courage*

RED-EYED ... Diana with Mirzeta yesterday

LOVE THAT MADE Di WEEP

CRUSADING Di sobbed yesterday as she comforted a Bosnian schoolgirl crippled by landmines.

The Princess burst into tears when she saw a charm round Mirzeta Gabelic's neck bearing the word: "Love."

It was a poignant message, coming

TURN TO PAGE TWO

Daily Record

Tuesday, August 12, 1997   28p

SCOTLAND'S CHAMPION

Petrol up by 27p a gallon

PETROL prices are set to soar by up to 27p a gallon, experts warned yesterday.

Cut-throat competition between garages has been keeping prices low, with only half of the Budget's 4p per litre duty increase passed on to drivers so far.

But industry experts reckon the full tax hike is about to go on pump prices, which will be pushed even higher by rises in crude oil and international petrol prices.

The oil companies yesterday admitted a rise was likely.

A BP spokesman said: "Profit margins are wafer thin."

Bosses at fleet services company **PHH Allstar**, which monitors fuel costs for 750,000 company vehicles, are convinced petrol is about to get dearer.

A spokesman said: "We anticipate a rise sometime later this month."

Kylie: My love for Stephane

COMEBACK queen Kylie Minogue revealed yesterday how her love for French photographer Stephane Sednaoui has helped put her career back on track.
FULL STORY – Pages 12 and 13

HEARTBREAK: Samantha survives on one biscuit a day

BRITAIN'S YOUNGEST ANOREXIC AGED 5

A GIRL aged just FIVE is being treated for anorexia.

Little Samantha Stephen is Britain's youngest victim of the disease.

She eats only one dry biscuit per day. Energy drinks keep her alive.

By STEVE SMITH

Samantha's frantic dad Gary, of Aberdeen, said last night: "We can't understand how this has happened to our little girl. It's breaking our hearts."

Samantha weighs just over

two stone. She is being treated for the symptoms of anorexia by psychiatrists at Royal Aberdeen Children's Hospital.

Gary, 34, said Sam's eating problems began when she was a year old. He added: "We've

TURN TO PAGE FOUR

FOOD FEAR ... tragic Samantha

Home RECORD 32 PAGES OF PROPERTY

111

Daily Record

Saturday, August 16, 1997 · 28p

SCOTLAND'S CHAMPION

Helen killed by Mad Cow disease

EXCLUSIVE

By ROGER HANNAH

A SCOTS OAP has become the latest victim of the human form of Mad Cow Disease.

The funeral of great-gran Helen Harris, 63, will take place today.

Her death came as the Government launched a new probe into Creutzfeldt-Jakob Disease and Britain's eating habits in the 80s.

Last night, Helen's heart

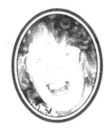

VICTIM ... Helen

broken family spoke of her battle against the illness

Daughter Margaret Walker, 27, said: "I never want to see anyone suffer like that again.

"She lost her sight, she forgot how to eat and forgot how to go to the toilet.

"This dreadful disease eats away the parts of the brain which send signals to other parts of the body.

"One day we found her unconscious on the kitchen floor – two months later she was dead.

"Latterly, she didn't know us and shook so violently she even threw herself off her bed on one occasion."

And Margaret revealed:

TURN TO PAGE 7

BESOTTED: *Princess ignores 'engagement' row*

DEFIANT DIANA STANDS BY DODI

DUCKING FOR COVER ... Di dashes from her Earls Court gym yesterday

PRINCESS Diana has vowed to stand by playboy lover Dodi Fayed.

She's brushed aside claims that the Harrods heir promised to wed Di-lookalike Kelly Fisher.

The princess believes their love can thrive despite Fisher's multi-million dollar lawsuit against Dodi.

By JAMES WHITAKER

"If she thinks about Fisher at all, she will view her as a troublemaker who is trying to make money out of her friendship with Dodi," said a friend.

Diana jetted out of the limelight yesterday for a yachting holiday in the Mediterranean with pal Rosa Monkton.

She was whisked away on Mohammed Al Fayed's personal

TURN TO PAGE THREE

RIVAL LOST FIRST LOVE TO MADONNA ~ Pages 2 & 3

Daily Record

Tuesday, August 19, 1997   28p

SCOTLAND'S CHAMPION

SMEAR ROW MP FACES BOOT

LABOUR are to suspend MP Tommy Graham over muck-spreading allegations.

Prime Minister Tony Blair last night ordered immediate disciplinary action against the West Renfrewshire MP.

He is accused of spreading malicious rumours about suicide MP Gordon McMaster. An announcement is expected in the next 24 hours.

Blair's move is seen as a bid to stop the sleaze row overshadowing Labour's drive for a Yes Yes vote at the devo referendum.

FULL STORY ~ PAGE 4

Tons of putrid pet food meat is sold to humans

By JAN DISLEY

THOUSANDS of people may have eaten rotten meat meant for pets in a sick food scam.

High Street discount chain Kwik Save – who have 75 shops in Scotland – were among those allegedly conned by dodgy butchers.

Meat traders passed off hundreds of tons of condemned chicken and turkey breasts as prime cuts.

Health chiefs believe the poultry could have been carrying killer bugs like E Coli, listeria and salmonella.

They fear hundreds of people may have fallen ill after eating it.

Slime

The alleged £3million fraud was uncovered after a probe by environmental health officers, which led to 37 arrests.

The unfit meat is no longer for sale.

A source close to the investigation said: "When one of our men saw what had happened to this meat, he had to go outside to be sick."

Chickens and turkeys which had been declared unfit for human consumption should have been minced up and used for pet food.

But workers were allegedly ordered to trim off the breasts and pack them separately in trays.

It's claimed they had to wash off "green slime" in huge salt baths, remove obvious bad bits and may

TURN TO PAGE SIX

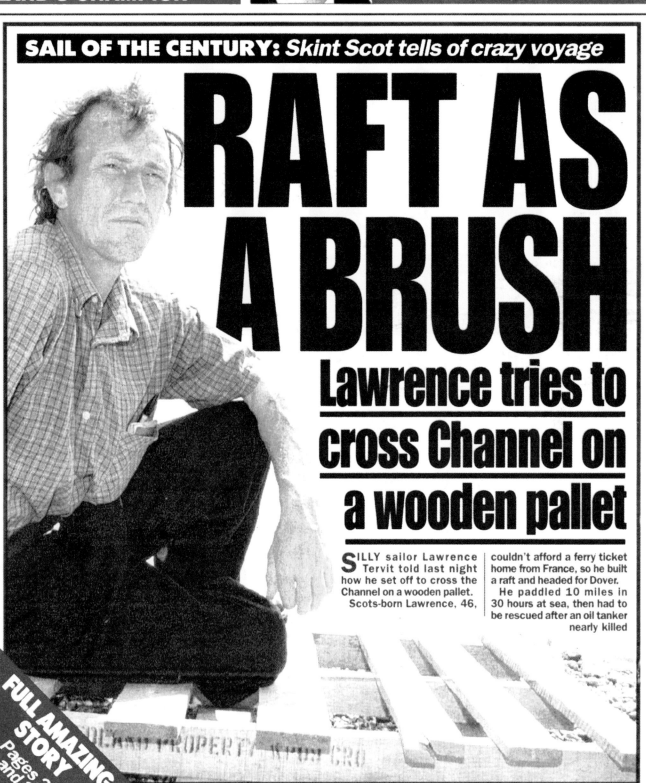

SAIL OF THE CENTURY: *Skint Scot tells of crazy voyage*

RAFT AS A BRUSH

Lawrence tries to cross Channel on a wooden pallet

SILLY sailor Lawrence Tervit told last night how he set off to cross the Channel on a wooden pallet.

Scots-born Lawrence, 46, couldn't afford a ferry ticket home from France, so he built a raft and headed for Dover.

He paddled 10 miles in 30 hours at sea, then had to be rescued after an oil tanker nearly killed

FULL AMAZING STORY Pages 2 and 3

GORAM: MY RANGERS BOOZE-UPS   PAGES 38&39

Daily Record

Wednesday, August 20, 1997   28p

SCOTLAND'S CHAMPION

TEARS OF SCHOOL'S LOCKOUT VICTIM, 5

– See Page 21

Liam lays into Spice Girls

By MATTHEW WRIGHT

ROCK wild man Liam Gallagher put the boot into the Spice Girls again yesterday.

The Oasis singer said the only people who cared about them were little kids.

And Liam, holidaying in sun-soaked St Tropez on the French Riviera with wife Patsy Kensit, said he couldn't give a damn about their music.

He added: "The Spice Girls might be a phenomenon.

"But they are simply not musically important to me or anyone else.

"The only people who care about the Spice Girls are four-year-old girls.

"Their music is nothing. They are a pre-fabricated pop product."

The superstar's latest outburst in the war of words with the Spice Girls follows an interview with Sporty Spice Mel C last week.

She laughed off a boast by Liam's guitarist brother, Noel, that Oasis were bigger than God.

She said: "What does

TURN TO PAGE THREE

Labour set up a hit squad to stop the rot as MP Graham admits: Yes, I am banned

SLEAZE BUSTERS

By KENNY FARQUHARSON

LABOUR chiefs last night sent a taskforce into Renfrewshire to stamp out sleaze once and for all.

The crackdown came as under-fire Renfrewshire West MP Tommy Graham admitted he'd been suspended from the parliamentary party.

His ban will last until the TURN TO PAGE FOUR

2 FREE GOES ON THE MIDWEEK LOTTO

CHANCE A `01 07 11 31 42 45`

CHANCE B `05 14 17 21 32 41`

AUG 20

PAGE 29

114

Daily Record

Tuesday, August 26, 1997

28p

SCOTLAND'S CHAMPION

Maggie ducks devo debate

IRON Lady Margaret Thatcher has chickened out of the Scottish Devolution debate.

The ex-Prime Minister is being paid a whopping £70,000 to give a one-hour speech in Glasgow – just two days before the

Devo referendum on September 11.

But she won't even mention Scotland's biggest political decision for decades.

Colleagues have convinced her that if she starts trumpeting her anti-Devo propaganda it will seriously hinder their No, No

TURN TO PAGE TWO

GO TO HELL: *Fed-up neighbours drive Haney out of town*

PACK YOUR BAGS MAGS

DEFIANT...Haney's two-fingered salute
Picture: JIM STEWART

NOTORIOUS Big Mags Haney was hounded out of her home last night.

The Mum from Hell gave a two-fingered salute to her relieved neighbours as she fled under police escort.

Almost 400 of them had staged a doorstep demo for more than an

By ALLISON McLAUGHLIN

hour in a bid to drive out the mum of eight and her family.

One of them said: "They caused so many problems with their violence and crime and we just wanted them out."

They got their wish just after 6pm, when peroxide blonde Mags – wearing

TURN TO PAGE THREE

115

Daily Record

Wednesday, August 27, 1997 — 28p

SCOTLAND'S CHAMPION

GREAT SCOTS RUN SPECIAL

Every name every result

16 Pages

STAR'S SCOTS SHAME

CHARLIE SHEEN IN COCAINE BENDER

HERO ... Wieghorst

Celtic win Euro thriller

CELTIC scored an amazing Euro triumph last night in a nine-goal thriller at Parkhead.

With just two minutes to go, Wim Jansen's men were heading out of the UEFA Cup on the away goals rule.

But Morten Wieghorst and Craig Burley scored in the dying minutes to give Celtic a famous victory.

They went through 7-5 on aggregate – sending the 47,000 Parkhead crowd wild.

But there was gloom on Tayside as Dundee United were held by Turkish side Trabzonspor and went out 2-1 on aggregate.

BACK PAGE

BRAVE... Helen Rollason

Beeb Helen's cancer fight

TELLY sports presenter Helen Rollason is battling cancer, it was revealed yesterday.

The 41-year-old – the first woman to host Grandstand – was admitted to hospital on Monday.

Doctors discovered a malignant tumour in her stomach and she's expected to have surgery in the next few days.

A BBC colleague said: "She's very determined and in a very positive frame of mind to fight it.

"She only found out on Monday and all of us here at the BBC are wishing her

TURN TO PAGE FIVE

HOT SHOT... Sheen struts on movie set at Clydebank

Daily Record EXCLUSIVE

MOVIE wildman Charlie Sheen blew nearly £1000 on a cocaine deal with a Scots hooker.

The hell-raising star peeled off 50-dollar bills as he pleaded drunkenly with the girl and her pimp to get him the drug.

Then he went with them in a taxi to close the deal in a notorious Glasgow housing scheme.

The taxi driver said: "I was amazed at Sheen. He seemed desperate for cocaine.

"He picked up this hooker off the street and told her he wanted coke. He was pulling wads of dollars out of his pockets.

"Half an hour later I'm sitting in Easterhouse with a movie star

By ANNA SMITH

in the back of my cab, and this hooker and her pimp handing him the bag of white powder."

Millionaire Sheen went on the drink and drug bender while filming his new film, Obit, in Glasgow.

Before taking the powder back to his hotel, he stopped at an all-night supermarket to buy tinfoil to test it out.

He also bought baking soda,

TURN TO PAGE TWO

CHANCE A .06 13 16 26 29 33   **CHANCE B** 04 19 27 30 39 43

AUG 27   **PAGE 27**

2 FREE GOES ON THE MIDWEEK LOTTO

LOUISE TOOK ME DIRTY DANCING

See Pages 28-29

SCOTS ACE IN BRAIN SCARE

DEVASTATED ... Darren faces more hospital tests

SCOTLAND striker Darren Jackson has a serious brain disorder, it was revealed last night.

The Celtic ace had a brain scan yesterday after complaining of a blinding headache.

It revealed a problem which will need an operation and may stop him ever playing again.

Darren, 31, missed Celtic's midweek Euro win because of the headache.

He thought it was a migraine but club doctor Jack Mulhearn arranged the scan as a precaution.

It's understood the former Hibs

Scan agony of Darren

By GORDON SIMPSON

and Dundee United hero is being treated at Ross Hall private hospital in Glasgow.

Doctors there are hopeful they can operate successfully.

Celtic general manager Jock Brown said: "Darren's condition is not life-threatening but may well be career-threatening.

"He is understandably demoralised."

FULL STORY ~ Back Page

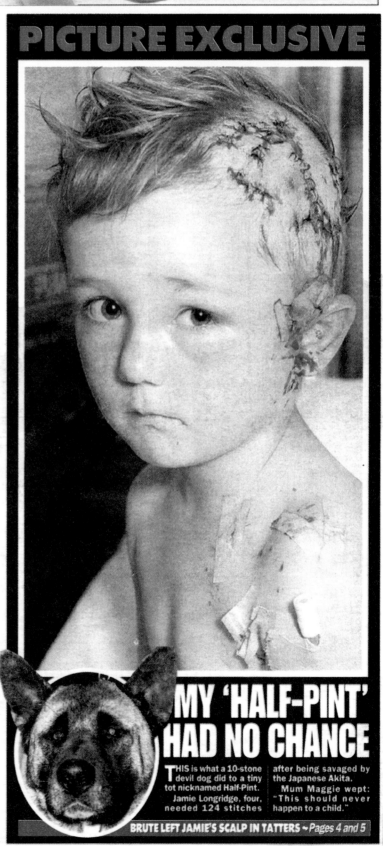

PICTURE EXCLUSIVE

MY 'HALF-PINT' HAD NO CHANCE

THIS is what a 10-stone devil dog did to a tiny tot nicknamed Half-Pint. Jamie Longridge, four, needed 124 stitches after being savaged by the Japanese Akita.

Mum Maggie wept: "This should never happen to a child."

BRUTE LEFT JAMIE'S SCALP IN TATTERS ~ Pages 4 and 5

sunday mail

55p August 31, 1997 4149

DIANA DEAD

PRINCESS DIANA IS DEAD. She died in the early hours of this morning after a horror car crash in Paris. Also killed was her lover Dodi Fayed.

● *FULL STORY PAGES 2 AND 3*

6am NEWS... KILLED WITH DODI IN CRASH

SAUDI NURSES SHOCKER

THE mother of Saudi murder case nurse Lucy McLauchlan spoke last night of her heartbreak.

Ann McLauchlan broke down over reports that one nurse will be beheaded and the other, her daughter, will face life in jail.

She spoke to the Mail after hearing the news that her

FULL STORY Pages 4 and 5

daughter had been found guilty of helping English colleague Deborah Parry to murder Aussie nurse Yvonne Gilford.

Lucy's mum heard reports that Parry was to be beheaded and that her daughter faced 20 years in a Saudi hell-hole.

Ann, 49, of Dundee, who has

just returned from visiting Lucy, sobbed: "We firmly believed to hear that Lucy would be coming home.

"I'm just shattered and can't take it in."

However, British lawyers representing the two accused nurses later denied that any judgment had been issued and that the reports were "without foundation."

FREE FILM

PLUS FREE DEVELOPING

Page 27

She lives alone with her cats, crying over a murdered pal and haunted by her past...

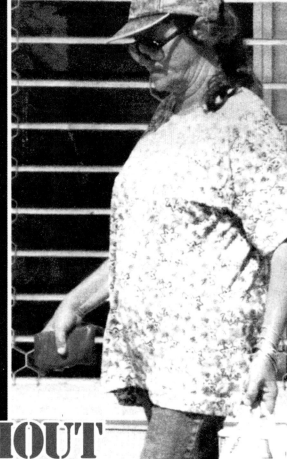

LIFE WITHOUT BILLY

by Iris Connolly

CENTRE PAGES

sunday mail

55p   August 31, 1997   4149

OLD FIRM CROWDS SHOCKER

Back page

GUILTY!

GUILTY... Lucy McLauchlan gets 20 years in jail

GUILTY... Deborah Parry faces a death sentence

Saudi nurse sentenced to death...

TWO British nurses were yesterday found guilty of the brutal killing of colleague Yvonne Gilford. Evil Deborah Parry has been sentenced to death and Scots nurse Lucy McLauchlan faces 20 years in a Saudi hell-hole jail.

LAST night McLauchlan's shattered mum Ann, 49, sobbed: "We weren't expecting this. We believed Lucy would soon be coming home to us." Australian Yvonne, 55, was stabbed 13 times, beaten and suffocated in the horror attack last December.

Full story-Pages 4 and 5

120

sunday mail

55p   *August 31, 1997*

Diana is dead

In the early hours of this morning Princess Diana died in a horror car crash in Paris, also killed was her new love Dodi Fayed

The life and times of a Princess... a Sunday Mail tribute

Daily Record

28p **SPECIAL EDITION**

Monday, Sept 1 1997

DIANA
Queen of broken hearts

In Loving Memory – Diana, Princess of Wales 1961-1997

Daily Record

Tuesday, September 2, 1997   28p

SCOTLAND MOURNS

NATION STANDS STILL

BRITAIN will come to a standstill on Saturday as Diana is laid to rest.

Millions will observe a tearful two-minute silence at 11am, when her funeral begins at Westminster Abbey.

Shops, pubs, businesses and tourist attractions like Edinburgh Castle will stay closed.

Even the National Lottery draw will be postponed out of respect.

GO AHEAD ... Queen

And the Braemar Gathering near Balmoral was cancelled late last night, hours after the Queen shocked locals by giving organisers her blessing to go ahead.

But Scotland's World Cup qualifier against Belarus at Pittodrie is expected to kick off as planned, even though all Saturday's matches in England and Wales have been axed.

FULL STORY ~ Pages 4 &5

Minder's 121mph madness

DIANA'S DRIVER WAS DRUNK

By BILL CAVEN

THE man who drove Princess Diana to her death was DRUNK.

Security guard Henri Paul was three and a half times the legal limit when he hurtled into a concrete pillar in a Paris tunnel, said officials.

Insiders revealed he was doing 121mph at the moment of impact.

And just before whisking Di and lover Dodi

TURN TO PAGE TWO

21-PAGE NEWS SPECIAL

Daily Record

Wednesday, September 3, 1997   28p

SCOTLAND'S CHAMPION

Elton to sing at Di funeral

ELTON JOHN is to sing a heart-rending tribute to Diana at her funeral, it was revealed yesterday.

The pop legend has been asked to perform Your Song as a fitting farewell to the Princess at the service in Westminster Abbey.

It was decided to invite him because of his close **TURN TO PAGE FOUR**

RECORD'S PLEA TO SFA SHABBY SEVEN..CALL THE BIG GAME OFF

| DOUG SMITH | CAMPBELL OGILVIE | IAN DONALD | DOUGLAS CROMB | GEORGE PEAT | JOHN McBETH | JACK McGINN |

SHAME ON YOU!

By STEPHEN RAFFERTY

HEARTLESS football bosses brought shame on Scotland yesterday.

They gave the go-ahead for a World Cup match on the day of Diana's funeral.

It will kick off just before the People's Princess is laid to rest.

But last night it was believed that some of Scotland's top stars are prepared to boycott the big game.

A senior player said: "What's the point when your heart's not in it."

Most of Britain will come to a standstill on Saturday.

Rugby, racing and English football matches have all been axed.

Shops and businesses across the country will close and the Lottery is being put back 24 hours.

But four hours after the funeral service at Westminster Abbey – and just before the private burial at Diana's family estate – Scotland will kick off against Belarus.

The decision, by seven of the SFA's International Committee, was condemned last night by fans.

And Scots Secretary Donald Dewar has been in touch with the

TURN TO PAGE NINE

Face of the drunk driver

THIS is the man who was behind the wheel of the Di and Dodi death crash.

Henri Paul, 41, was more than three times the limit when their Mercedes ploughed into a concrete pillar in a Paris road tunnel.

And last night it was revealed that Paul was a speed freak who regularly enjoyed marathon booze sessions. **FULL STORY – Pages 2 & 3**

CINDY CRAWFORD KEPT DODI LOVE SECRET FOR 9 MONTHS–Pages 6 and 7

Daily Record

Thursday, September 4, 1997   28p

SCOTLAND'S CHAMPION

I GIVE DIANA BACK TO GOD WITH PRIDE

MUM'S SORROW ~ Pages 8 and 9

LOVE TOKEN ... Dodi

Princess died with ring Dodi gave her

By TED OLIVER and DON MACKAY

PRINCESS Diana was given a fabulous ring by boyfriend Dodi Fayed hours before they both died.

It was found in the death car with the couple, who were on the brink of announcing their engagement.

Harrods heir Dodi had planned the final stages of wooing Diana – a romantic dinner at his father's Paris Ritz Hotel, then champagne at his luxury apartment.

They were on the way to the flat near the Arc de Triomphe when they crashed.

Dodi chose the ring "on approval" from jewellers Alexandre Reza on Saturday morning, after returning with Diana from holiday in Sardinia.

Diamonds

Staff at Reza's would not comment last night. But a source at a top Paris gem dealers confirmed the purchase.

He said: "It is the talk of the trade here. We have heard it was diamonds and worth a fortune."

It is believed the firm lodged an insurance claim for the value of the ring soon after Sunday's crash.

But they withdrew it when the ring, still in its box, was recovered from the wreckage of the Mercedes limousine.

It was handed to Diana's sister Sarah with the rest of her possessions, and was thought to be at Kensington Palace last night.

A family friend said: "This was the real thing. It's so heart-breaking.

"Dodi gave her the ring that day, only a short while before they died."

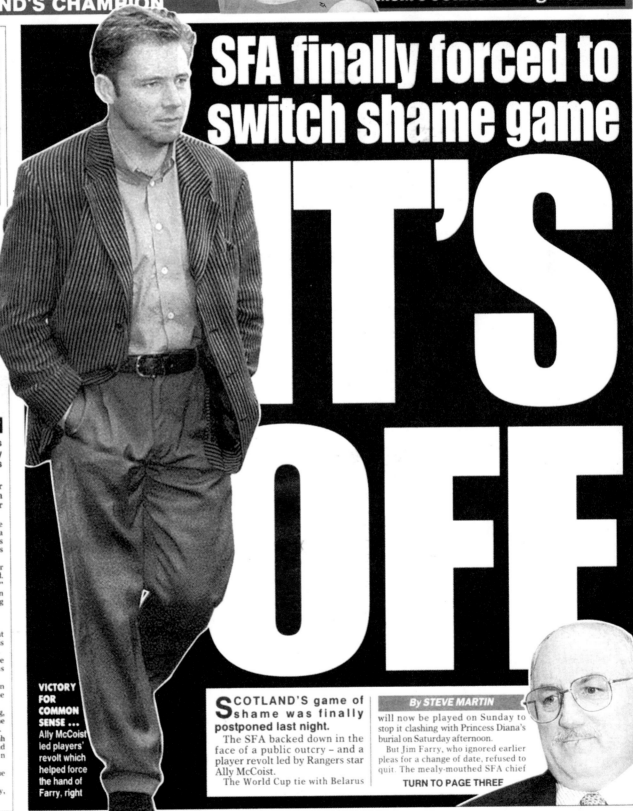

VICTORY FOR COMMON SENSE ... Ally McCoist led players' revolt which helped force the hand of Farry, right

SFA finally forced to switch shame game

IT'S OFF

SCOTLAND'S game of shame was finally postponed last night.

The SFA backed down in the face of a public outcry – and a player revolt led by Rangers star Ally McCoist.

The World Cup tie with Belarus

By STEVE MARTIN

will now be played on Sunday to stop it clashing with Princess Diana's burial on Saturday afternoon.

But Jim Farry, who ignored earlier pleas for a change of date, refused to quit. The mealy-mouthed SFA chief

TURN TO PAGE THREE

HARRY BEGS TO MARCH AT FUNERAL
Pages 4 & 5

125

CHARLES COMFORTS GRIEF-STRICKEN HARRY

Daily Record

Friday, September 5, 1997   28p

SCOTLAND'S CHAMPION

HOLD MY HAND DADDY

DADDY'S BOY ... Charles holds Harry's hand while Wills reads tributes at Crathie

By CHARLIE GALL

HEARTBROKEN Prince Harry clung to his dad's hand last night as he read how much the nation loved his mum.

Prince Charles, Harry, 12, and brother William, 15, spent a poignant few minutes at the gates of Balmoral looking at tributes to Princess Diana left by mourners.

The letter Harry read said: "I hope the young princes will stand strong and proud."

FULL STORY ~ *Pages Two and Three*

'HURT' QUEEN TO ADDRESS NATION: *Pages Four and Five*

Mother Teresa is dead

CENTRE PAGES

Daily Record

Saturday, September 6, 1997 — 28p

NATION SAYS FAREWELL

Di will never be forgotten

●THE Queen yesterday paid heartfelt tribute to Diana in an unprecedented television address to the nation. She said the princess was an 'exceptional and gifted human being' who would never be forgotten.

PAGES 4 and 5

PEOPLE'S PRINCES

TENDER TOUCHES ... Prince William reaches out to crowds at Kensington Palace while Harry, left, hugs a mourner

INSIDE: 24-PAGE GUIDE TO THE FUNERAL

The world says farewell

Daily Record

Monday, September 8, 1997   28p

SCOTLAND'S CHAMPION

PM'S PLEA FROM THE HEART

YES!

Build better Britain for Di

YES!

Vote for bright new Scotland

RECORD VIEW

SCOTLAND sets aside its sorrow today as we turn to the historic decision on our own future.

Prime Minister Tony Blair, in an exclusive Daily Record interview, urges Scots: "Grieve for Diana – but seize the chance of a new life for Scotland."

In a heartfelt plea to the British public, he called on everyone to help build a better, more compassionate Britain as a lasting legacy to Diana.

And he called on every Scot to ensure that Thursday's referendum

TURN TO PAGE FIVE

INSIDE TODAY

32-PAGE MEMORIAL   *Daily Record*   SEPTEMBER 8, 1997

The world says farewell

● IT was Britain's saddest day – the funeral of Diana, Princess of Wales. Today the people's paper publishes a 32-page full-colour memorial to the People's Princess.

Princess buried with Mother Teresa rosary

By JANE KERR

PRINCESS DI was buried with a treasured rosary given to her by missionary nun Mother Teresa.

Di carried them everywhere and they were recovered at the La Pitie-Salpetriere hospital where she lost her fight for life after the Paris car crash.

The fashion-leading princess was laid to rest in a long-sleeved black designer dress.

She bought the coat-

dress, by her favourite designer Catherine Walker, just four weeks ago – but never had the chance to wear it.

A love poem to her by Dodi Fayed, inscribed on a silver plaque, may also have gone into her coffin.

The plaque was found under Di's pillow in the Paris apartment where she had been staying.

Dodi's father Mohamed

TURN TO PAGE TWO

Daily Record

Friday, September 12, 1997   **28p**

SCOTLAND'S CHAMPION

A NEW DAWN

Scotland wakes up to People's Parliament

DEWAR LEADS THE WAY 2&3 • BRAVEHEARTS ON MARCH 4&5

Daily Record

Friday, September 12, 1997 — 28p

SCOTLAND'S CHAMPION

6AM VICTORY SPECIAL

YES 74% FOR SCOTTISH PARLIAMENT YES 63% VOTE FOR TAX POWERS

Daily Record

Saturday, September 13, 1997   28p

SCOTLAND'S CHAMPION

FAN POWER FORCES BIG GAME SWITCH

Back page

PM TONY BLAIR SAYS..

YOU CAN'T BEAT *Record*

YES! YES!

READERS!

GRATEFUL Tony Blair thanked Daily Record readers last night for winning Scotland a Parliament.

The Premier, celebrating the historic Devo victory, said: "Such a tremendous result would have been very difficult without the constant and dedicated support of the Daily Record."

By DAVE KING

Blair was one of a string of political leaders to praise the part you played in making the Devo dream come true.

Scots Secretary Donald Dewar said: "There is no doubt the Record made a critical difference, not just in the last four weeks but TURN TO PAGE THREE

PARTY CHIEFS PRAISE YOUR PART IN DEVO TRIUMPH

Daily Record

Tuesday, September 16, 1997   28p

SCOTLAND'S CHAMPION

X APPEAL
GILLIAN IS BEST ACTRESS
FULL STORY–Pages 20 & 21

Police swoop grabs Tubby fakes

By TONY ELLIN

FAKE Teletubby goods have been seized in a raid by trading standards.

Officers grabbed unlicensed T-shirts, key-rings and stickers from five cash-and-carry stores on Glasgow's south side.

The swoop came as the BBC warned parents that imitation Teletubby products could be dangerous.

A spokesman said: "Some of the counterfeit goods seized are potentially lethal.

"One Teletubby doll was stuffed with straw. If this came near a naked flame, there would be an inferno. Our

WANTED ... Po

primary concern is for safety because this is a programme for young children."

A Glasgow City Council spokesman said the seized goods would be destroyed.

In a separate move, the BBC have threatened to take action against Glasgow company Clyde Importers amid claims that they sold fakes.

A spokeswoman said: "We are looking into the activities of this company and have asked trading standards officers to investigate."

Demand for official Teletubby products has been phenomenal.

Shops sold out of the new range within hours last week and parents have been queuing up to get their hands on the toys.

Stars of the show – Po, Laa Laa, Tinky Winky and Dipsy – have also become cult stars with students.

EXCLUSIVE

Candlestick killer Louise breaks vow of silence

CANDLESTICK killer Louise Clark has broken her silence and revealed: "I'll always love the man I battered to death." Louise, 21, suffered horrific abuse from boyfriend Ed Giles, 43.

TURN TO PAGES 10 & 11

PALACE ATTACK: *Newsman Snow under fire*

QUEEN SLAMS TV LIES

By ADRIAN SHAW

UNDER FIRE ... Jon Snow of Channel 4

THE Queen launched a bitter and thinly-veiled attack on Channel 4 newsman Jon Snow yesterday.

She hit back over his claim that she had tried to order a low-key private funeral for Princess Diana.

And she said his report of behind-the-scenes rows about the service were "the direct opposite of the truth".

A statement from Buckingham Palace did not mention Snow by name – but royal sources insisted he was being singled out for her wrath.

Snow claimed on Channel 4 News last week that the Queen did not want a public funeral.

He said she had ordered Diana's body to be held in a private mortuary and "under no circumstances" be taken to a royal palace.

Snow's report also said Prince Charles had a stand-up row over

TURN TO PAGE TWO

---

36 PAGES OF PROPERTY INSIDE

Daily Record

Thursday, September 18, 1997   28p

SCOTLAND'S CHAMPION

PLAY £25,000 **INSTANT SCRATCH** PAGE 37

TOP JOB ... Zoe

Zoe lands Radio 1 hot seat

STUNNING kids TV star Zoe Ball is to take over the Radio 1 Breakfast Show.

The blonde beauty becomes the first ever woman to land the most prestigious job in British radio.

Zoe, 26, has signed a £150,000 contract and will co-host the early morning slot with Kevin Greening

A pal said last night: "She is absolutely delighted. It's a dream come true. She'll be celebrating like mad."

FULL STORY ~ Page 3

CRUSADE...Blair

Labour's kiss of life for nurses

TONY Blair plans a massive crusade to rescue Britain's nurses from despair.

The alarmed Premier has ordered urgent action to combat the crisis of morale in hospitals.

He wants to halt the tide of nurses quitting the job because of stress, low prestige and the threat of violence from patients.

The job would carry more skills and respect, fit in better

TURN TO PAGE 2

TV CHICK'S TEARS FOR DEATH SMASH BOY

ESCAPED...Keith Young with girlfriend Linda Martin

Son is cut free from wreckage

TELLY pundit Chick Young wept yesterday as he talked about the crash which injured his son and killed one of his pals.

Keith Young, 17, was on his way home with three friends when his car ploughed into a tree. He had to be cut

By VIVIENNE AITKEN

free from the wreckage. Chick, who kept a 24-hour vigil at his son's bedside, sobbed: "I am totally devastated.

"My thoughts are with the mum and dad of the young boy who was killed."

FULL STORY PAGE SEVEN

Kirsty saved my life

IT'S ON

HELLRAISER Donovan Leitch has told how Scots beauty Kirsty Hume saved his life.

The son of flower-power singer Donovan spoke on the eve of his romantic Loch Lomond-side wedding to the blonde supermodel.

The couple went through a rehearsal yesterday. Kirsty kept supercool as ever – and even took time out to comfort a weeping pal.

PAGE THREE

Edwina ditches hubby

IT'S OVER

FORMER Tory motor-mouth Edwina Currie has split from her husband after 25 years.

She dumped 52-year-old Ray after he refused to move to London where the ex-MP now writes bonkbuster novels.

Edwina revealed the split in Glasgow yesterday, where she is promoting her new book. It's called She's Leaving Home!

PAGE EIGHT

SHAME OF HEARTLESS HUSBAND

DUMP MY WIFE IN PAUPER GRAVE

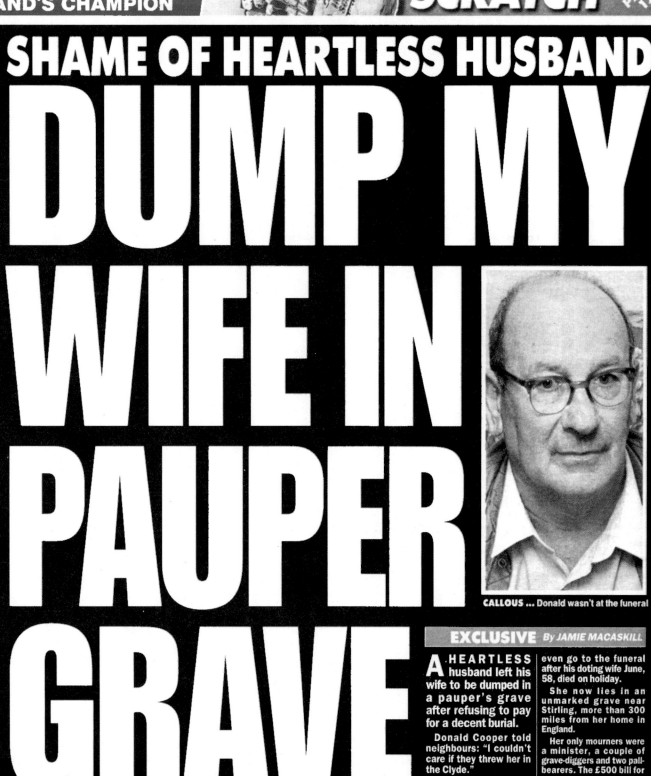

CALLOUS ... Donald wasn't at the funeral

EXCLUSIVE By JAMIE MACASKILL

A HEARTLESS husband left his wife to be dumped in a pauper's grave after refusing to pay for a decent burial.

Donald Cooper told neighbours: "I couldn't care if they threw her in the Clyde."

Callous Cooper didn't even go to the funeral after his doting wife June, 58, died on holiday.

She now lies in an unmarked grave near Stirling, more than 300 miles from her home in England.

Her only mourners were a minister, a couple of grave-diggers and two pall-bearers. The £500 bill for

TURN TO PAGE NINE

HOME RECORD - 40 PAGES OF PROPERTY INSIDE

Daily Record

LIVING LIFE TO THE MAX!

BIGGAR SMALLAR!

WE'RE MAKING THE BIG YINS OF

INSIDE THE MAX!

YOUR NEW WEEKLY GUIDE TO FITNESS AND HEALTH

Wednesday, September 24, 1997   28P

SCOTLAND'S CHAMPION

BRIDE AND HUME

SCOTS supermodel Kirsty Hume was a beautiful bride on the Bonnie Banks yesterday. The Ayrshire beauty wed Donovan Leitch on Loch Lomondside ... after keeping him waiting half an hour.

MAID OF THE LOCH – Pages 26 & 27

Family's plea to world

SAVE OUR LUCY

ORDEAL... nurse Lucy faces agony of public flogging

By BRIAN McCARTNEY

THE parents of the Scots nurse sentenced to FIVE HUNDRED lashes in Saudi Arabia begged the world to save her last night.

Lucy McLauchlan, 31, from Dundee, also faces eight years in a hellhole prison after a Moslem court ruled she was an accessory to a colleague's murder.

Her friend and fellow-nurse Deborah Parry, 38, could be publicly beheaded if reports she has been found guilty of the killing are confirmed.

Lucy's anguished dad Stan called the verdict against her "unbelievable". He said there was "not a shred of evidence" to back it up.

Stan, 50, said he would beg Prime Minister Tony

TURN TO PAGE THREE

● **Saudis sentence Scot to 500 lashes**
● **Her nurse pal could be beheaded**

Daily Record

Thursday, September 25, 1997   28p

SCOTLAND'S CHAMPION

TARGET... Monty

Monty to get armed guard at Cup

By STEVE MILLAR

ARMED guards will protect Scotland's top golfer Colin Montgomerie from a terrorist threat at the Ryder Cup.

Police in Spain fear Monty and America's Tiger Woods will be targeted by Basque fanatics during the showdown between Europe and the USA.

Monty and Tiger, two of the biggest stars on show, are being classed as major risks. They will get an armed guard starting today.

Alert

Sixteen British soldiers have volunteered to shadow the two players at the Valderrama course.

Spain has been on heightened terror alert since Basque separatist group ETA shot and killed a young politician earlier this year.

Thirty thousand fans are expected to see the cup tee off tomorrow.

Crack troops have been ordered to guard entry points to the course. Spain's Civil Guard and armed and mounted police will also be on duty.

Ryder Cup chiefs have posted 750 marshals around the course to weed out drunken louts.

RYDER CUP LATEST ~ Pages 57, 58 & 59

Brother demands blood money

£750,000 OR DEBBIE DIES!

DRIVING A DEADLY BARGAIN ... greedy Gilford yesterday

A £750,000 price has been put on the head of murder charge nurse Deborah Parry.

The brother of victim Yvonne Gilford is set to pocket almost £450,000 from the blood money deal.

Frank Gilford, 59, has signed a secret agreement with the defence to waive his legal right to demand Deborah's execution.

By ANNA SMITH and IAIN FERGUSON

Deborah, 38, of Hampshire, denies murdering her colleague Yvonne.

But unconfirmed reports from Saudi suggest she has been found guilty and could face public beheading.

Deborah's co-accused Lucy McLauchlan, from Dundee, has

TURN TO PAGE FIVE

THREAT... Deborah

INSIDE: 16 PAGES OF JOBS / £25,000 INSTANT SCRATCH

137

Pawn shops fund new Lotto boom

LOTTO Scots went pawn crackers yesterday...

As punters queued at PAWN SHOPS to raise cash in a bid to land the estimated £30 MILLION double rollover jackpot.

Hopefuls raided their lofts to swap valuables for Lotto tickets.

And they forked out a staggering £75 million throughout the UK in a last-minute scramble to land the massive prize.

Pawn shops all over Scotland reported takings up around 20 per cent...

One woman even pawned her granny's antique gold chain for just £100 in the hope of the big money win last night.

FULL STORY — Page 5

BETRAYAL

Dunc vows: I won't play for Scotland ever again...

■ **FOOTBALL** star Duncan Ferguson has dropped a bombshell on his native country.

At just 28, the Everton striker has told Scotland boss Craig Brown that he NEVER wants to play for the national team again.

Ferguson's shock decision to walk out on an international career was made clear in a letter to the SFA.

FULL STORY – Back Page

SNUBBED ... Craig Brown

sunday mail

55p   *September 28, 1997*   *4153*

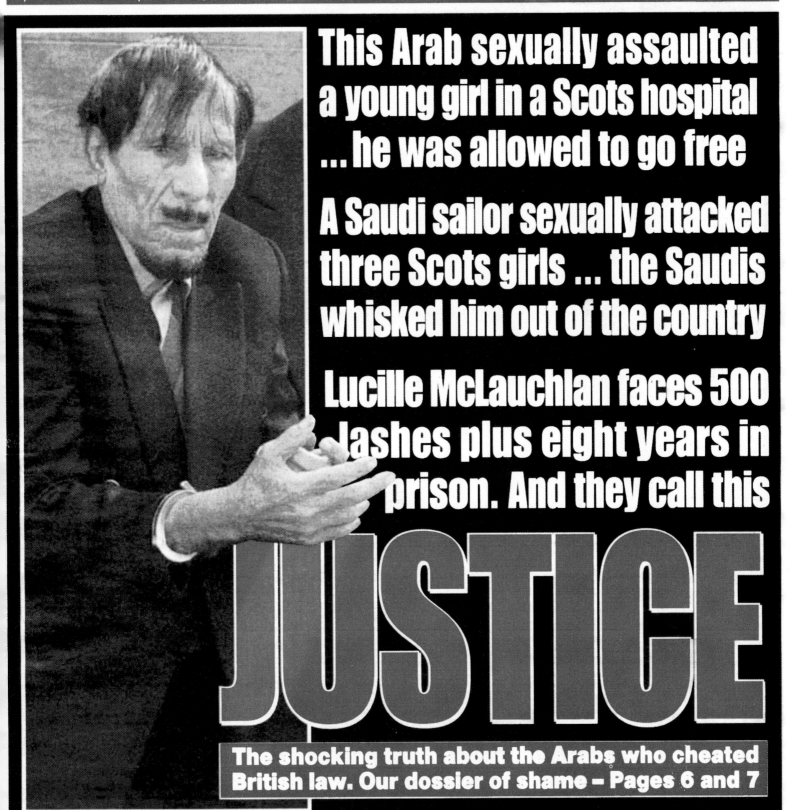

This Arab sexually assaulted a young girl in a Scots hospital ... he was allowed to go free

A Saudi sailor sexually attacked three Scots girls ... the Saudis whisked him out of the country

Lucille McLauchlan faces 500 lashes plus eight years in prison. And they call this

JUSTICE

The shocking truth about the Arabs who cheated British law. Our dossier of shame – Pages 6 and 7

Daily Record

Monday, September 29, 1997   30p

SCOTLAND'S CHAMPION

SAVE £129

TWO FOR ONE

TRAIN FARES

PAGE 14

TUM'S THE WORD
WOMAN SPECIAL
PAGES 16-17

THE COOL MONTY

COOL Colin Montgomerie was the toast of Europe last night after clinching golf's biggest prize – the Ryder Cup.

The big Scot sealed a superb one-point victory for Europe's underdogs over the high-powered USA, then beamed: "This is fantastic. It's what it's all about."

OLE GRAIL ~ Back Page

Three kids in drugs overdose

By JAMIE MACASKILL

THREE children were seriously ill in hospital early today after overdosing on drugs.

Two girls and a boy, aged between 10 and 12, swallowed handfuls of powerful pain-killers.

Ambulances rushed them to Paisley's Royal Alexandra Hospital from Blackstoun Oval in the town, a well-known hangout for teenagers.

Hospital staff were on emergency alert over fears that more youngsters could have been involved.

Police were shocked

TURN TO PAGE 2

Brown's jobs for all vow

IRON Chancellor Gordon Brown will today deliver a jobs-for-all-promise to the Labour Party faithful.

He will spell out his Millennium vision of full employment in his keynote speech to the Brighton conference.

Brown wants to put in place a system where job opportunities are guaranteed to those who want them.

And his dream could become reality after the year 2000 – thanks to Government plans to open up education and reform tax and benefits.

FULL STORY ~ Page Two

Daily Record

Tuesday, September 30, 1997   30p

SCOTLAND'S CHAMPION

PAGE 6

WE WON £11m BY MISTAKE

Pub pals put the same lottery line on TWICE

Hearts ace in probe over scuffle

EXCLUSIVE
By RAY NOTARANGELO

HEARTS ace Paul Ritchie was being questioned by police about an alleged scuffle outside a club.

Two men were injured in an incident at the Bowhill Miners' Welfare Club in Cardenden, Fife.

The former Scottish under-21 internationalist was later quizzed by police.

Trouble was believed to have started as Gary Calder, 17, and his brother Scott, 20, of Fife, were waiting in a taxi queue after leaving the club in the early hours of Sunday morning.

Wound

Ritchie, 22, who is from Kirkcaldy and joined the Edinburgh side in 1992, is understood to have been with fellow Hearts players celebrating Saturday's 3-0 victory over Kilmarnock.

Both brothers were taken to Kirkcaldy's Victoria Infirmary after the incident.

Scott was treated for an inch-long wound to the back of his head.

Gary suffered a black eye and had treatment for a wound on his forehead.

Fife police confirmed they were investigating an incident at the welfare club.

They said last night they were questioning several people.

BLOOD MONEY: *New book is insult to princess*

BETRAYAL!
Charles' anger as Di author cashes in

DIANA

Her True Story

ANDREW MORTON

AUTHOR ... Morton

ANGRY ... Charles

AUTHOR Andrew Morton was blasted by Prince Charles last night for "betraying" Diana.

The palace reacted with fury over Morton's claim that the

By STEPHEN WHITE

princess was the secret source for his book.

He's rushing out a new version of Diana, The True Story – insisting that it should be treated as her autobiography.

He says she authorised ALL the revelations about her bulimia and her husband's

adultery. But last night, friends of the prince accused the author of seeking blood money.

One said: "The prince will be very concerned about the effect this will have on William and Harry.

"It is only four weeks since their mother died and the last thing they need right now is Andrew Morton cashing in in such a disgusting way."

FULL STORY: *Pages 12 and 13*

Daily Record

Wednesday, October 1, 1997   30p

SCOTLAND'S CHAMPION

CARE FOR BRITAIN AND IT WILL CARE FOR YOU

BLAIR'S VISION FOR THE 21ST CENTURY: PAGES 2 & 3

Daily Record

Thursday, October 2, 1997 — 30p

SCOTLAND'S CHAMPION

Drunken blind man bites his guide dog

By GORDON McILWRAITH

A BLIND man BIT his guide dog in the street in a nasty drunken attack.

Faithful labrador Upton could not understand his master's slurred commands.

He was bitten on the nose and ears and punched by Charles Dubois, 33.

The scared dog – who was donated by charity – curled up during the five-minute assault which was caught on a closed circuit TV.

Police led 6ft 7in Dubois to the cells and Upton was taken off him.

A court later banned him for life from owning dogs. It's thought he was the first blind man in Britain to get such a severe punishment.

But appeal judges yesterday reduced the sentence.

FULL STORY PAGE 7

Sheriffs to run crooks off road

EXCLUSIVE

CRIMINALS are going to be run off the road by the courts.

Sheriffs will be given powers to impose bans for any crimes – not just driving offences.

The new laws are part of a pilot scheme to be tested at two sheriff courts from January 1.

But last night, the plan came under heavy attack.

A spokesman for the RAC said: "What sense does it make to ban a pickpocket from driving?

"Removing someone's licence can have catastrophic effects on their livelihood.

"And it can cause hardship to

TURN TO PAGE 5

FISHING BOAT CAPSIZES IN STORM

ALIVE

Skipper is pulled from sea as four crew drown

SO LUCKY ... Victor is taken to hospital after his ordeal

By STEVE SMITH, CHARLIE GALL and CARA PAGE

TRAWLER skipper Victor Robertson was plucked from the North Sea by a helicopter yesterday after his boat was sunk in a storm.

But his four crew were missing, feared drowned, after their Peterhead-based boat Sapphire was hit by a huge wave.

A massive air and sea search was called off until first light.

And last night, coastguards admitted they had all but given up hope of finding the men alive.

A spokesman said: "We don't think they could have survived in that water for more than four and half hours."

The Sapphire went down 20 miles off Peterhead.

Bachelor Victor, 27, who was

TURN TO PAGE FOUR

Daily Record

Friday, October 3, 1997 — 30p

SCOTLAND'S CHAMPION

FERGIE WEEPS FOR Di

PAGES 12 and 13

LIAM ... Christmas cracker

Oasis order double Scots

By JOHN DINGWALL

OASIS have lined up a Christmas cracker for Scotland.

The band will play two shows in Glasgow in December – as a thank you to fans.

Last night, songwriter Noel Gallagher said: "Scotland's a bit of alright.

"We always have a great time there."

The band, currently riding high in the charts with Stand By Me, will launch the second half of their UK tour at Glasgow's SECC on December 7 and 8.

Atmosphere

Ticket details will be finalised over the next few days. But they won't be on sale until the end of the month.

A spokesman for promoters Regular Music said: "It's brilliant that they've chosen to start things off in Glasgow.

"Being so close to Christmas, the atmosphere is going to be exceptional for the lucky fans who snap up tickets."

An Oasis insider admitted last night: "Noel and Liam are always going on about Scotland.

"They've never forgotten that they were signed there.

"That, and the fact that Creation boss Alan McGee is Scottish, means that the shows up there are among the best they've played.

"This will be no exception."

TRAGEDY: *Town of sorrow mourns lost fishermen*

SON IN A MILLION ... Bruce

YOUNGEST ABOARD ... Robert

FAMILY MAN ... Victor

THEY DIDN'T STAND A CHANCE

THE four victims of the Sapphire fishing tragedy had no chance to save themselves, it was revealed last night.

Rescuers said the only survivor, skipper Victor Robertson, told them his crew were all inside the Peterhead trawler when it was sunk by a freak wave.

Victor, right, managed to dive through the window of the wheelhouse as the boat capsized "as quickly as a handclap".

But Robert Stephen, 25, Adam Stephen, 29, Bruce Cameron, 32, and Victor Podlesny, 46, were dragged 250 feet to the seabed.

DON'T BLAME SKIPPER
Pages 2 and 3

INSIDE: 36 PAGES OF MOTORS / 2 FOR 1 RAIL TICKET OFFER PAGE 43

sunday mail

55p October 5. 1997 4154

OUTRAGE!

He killed a young Celtic fan...now the UVF has forced the Government to turn an evil thug into a Loyalist hero

EXCLUSIVE

THE vicious killer of a young Celtic fan is being moved to the Maze prison in Ulster – as a POLITICAL PRISONER.

Jason Campbell slashed the throat of 16-year-old Mark Scott two years ago and left him to die in the gutter in a busy Glasgow street.

Now Northern Ireland secretary Mo Mowlam has approved his transfer to the Maze, where he will be treated as a terrorist.

And the killer can look forward to special treatment under the auspices of the Ulster Volunteer Force.

FULL STORY – Page 2

Daily Record

Tuesday, October 7, 1997 — 30p

SCOTLAND'S CHAMPION

FLASHPOINT: *Is this Chic yob?*

MATCH STILL ... TV cameras capture the scene on the terracing

HURLING ... The fan appears to throw something from the crowd

TV clue to coin throw

THESE are the pictures which may help find the yob who threw a missile at Hibs star Chic Charnley.

They are taken from TV film which appears to show a Rangers fan throwing an object in the direction of the pitch during Saturday's match.

Charnley slumped to his knees and clutched his head during the seven-goal thriller with Rangers. The player claimed he had been struck by a missile thrown by Rangers fans housed in

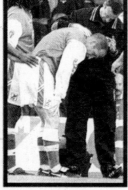

INJURY ... Chic gets treated

TURN TO PAGE 4

£2.8m LOTTERY WINNER CHARGES SON RENT

BUBBLY ... Liam, centre, toasts the win with his family

THE son of a lotto millionaire has been given 20 weeks to pay a £200 fine – after a sheriff heard his parents charge him RENT.

Liam Slattery, 19, coughs up £20 a week

By BILLY ADAMS

for bed and board even though dad John won £2.8million.

After paying his digs, the apprentice joiner only has £80 a week left.

His dad, who won the

TURN TO PAGE 6

FANS IN DARK AS ⑤ CLINCH SCOTS MATCH

BACK PAGE

Daily Record

Wednesday, October 8, 1997   FIRST   30p

SCOTLAND'S CHAMPION

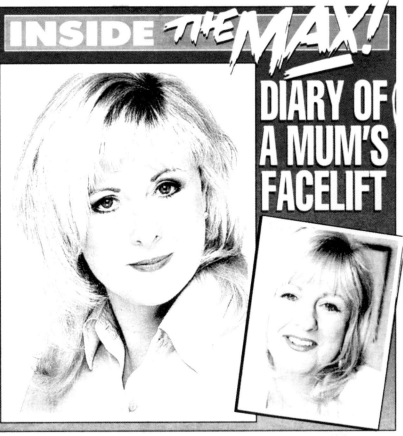

9 FREE GOES ON THE LOTTO

WINNER ... David

Jason scoops awards hat-trick

By TONY ELLIN

STAR actor David Jason scooped three top prizes at the National Television Awards last night.

He was voted Most Popular Comedy Performer and Most Popular Actor.

And his Only Fools And Horses Christmas '96 Special landed Most Popular Comedy.

It was a massive victory for Jason, 56, who won a Special Lifetime Achievement award at last year's bash.

Troubled Michael Barrymore marked the end of a nightmare year with Most Popular Entertainment Presenter.

And drag queen Lily Savage scooped Most Popular Entertainment Programme award for An Audience With show.

Stunning supermodel Caprice Bourret stole the limelight in a figure-hugging outfit at the Royal Albert Hall event.

TWO GIRLS UNDER HOUSE ARREST

CURFEW ... teenage tearaways Milne, left, and Taylor

TWO tearaway teenage girls were under HOUSE ARREST last night.

Christina Taylor, 16, and Samantha Milne, 17, were ordered to stay indoors after their drunken antics landed them in court.

Tough Sheriff Norrie Stein told them they'll go to prison if they break the 24-hour curfew.

The girls can't go out without their parents. They have vowed to accept their punishment.

FULL STORY ~ PAGE FIVE

Daily Record

Thursday, October 9, 1997   30p

SCOTLAND'S CHAMPION

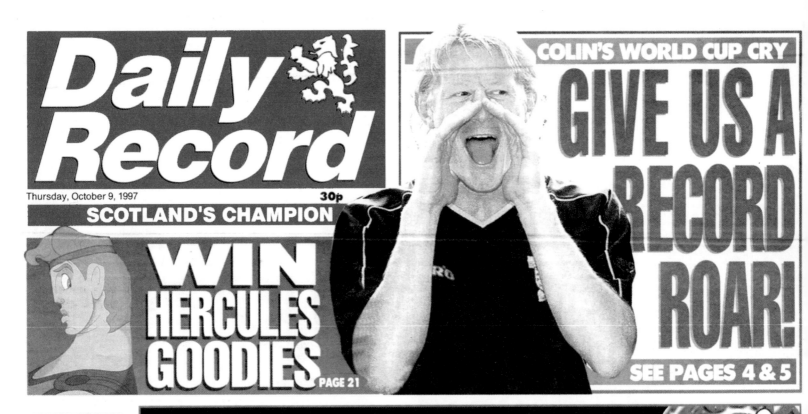

COLIN'S WORLD CUP CRY

GIVE US A RECORD ROAR!

SEE PAGES 4 & 5

WIN HERCULES GOODIES
PAGE 21

QUEEN... can't cope

I'M TOO OLD

Queen feels her 71 years

By JAMES WHITAKER

THE Queen admitted yesterday that she felt too old to cope with the modern world.

The monarch, who's 71, also said it was time for the "younger generation" to take the lead.

It was the first time the Queen, who's reigned for 45 years, has indicated she's feeling the strain of her age and her job.

In an astonishing speech, she said: "I sometimes sense that the world is changing far too fast for its inhabitants, at least for us older ones.

"It is the younger generation who must lead the way in fostering our friendship."

The Queen was speaking during her state visit

TURN TO PAGE TWO

Parents fight to axe law that frees child abusers

GIVE US JUSTICE

By JULIA CLARKE

TWO tormented Scots parents last night begged for a change to the law which lets hundreds of child sex beasts cheat justice.

Susan and Mark MacDonald told how courts refused to prosecute the fiend who abused their daughter Melanie, four.

The tot told in horrific detail what a teenage neighbour did to her.

But Scots law says her words are not enough to put the fiend on trial. Two independent pieces of evidence are needed.

In America, beasts can be prosecuted on a child's evidence, plus testimony from an expert.

The MacDonalds – not their real name – say Scots children are being denied justice.

Susan said: "I want the Record to highlight this gap in the law, before another childhood is ruined."

Anti-abuse campaigners are backing the family, in a bid to nail more perverts. Research shows just **ONE PER CENT** of Scots abuse cases end in convictions.

PICTURE POSED BY MODEL

INNOCENCE BETRAYED ~ *Centre Pages*

148

FLY TO LONDON FOR £12

Price excludes £10 airport tax

Daily Record

Friday, October 10, 1997   30p

SCOTLAND'S CHAMPION

DON'T MISS TOMORROW'S RECORD

Ina lied to hubby for 80 years

CRAFTY Ina Marshall thought she'd found the secret of eternal youth – until the Queen exposed her secret.

Ina lied to hubby John about her age for 80 years.

But the truth came out yesterday when she received a telegram from The Queen congratulating her on reaching 100.

PAGE 5

Flagging Maggie's plane daft

FLAGGING Maggie Thatcher got up to some hankie panky during a walkabout at the Tory conference yesterday.

She told off a British Airways director for dumping the Union Flag from their jets' tailplanes.

Then she pulled a hanky from her bag and wrapped it round the multi-coloured tail of a model plane.

PAGE 2

EXCLUSIVE: *Stab thug will serve sentence in Scotland*

DEWAR BLOCKS KILLER'S TRANSFER

KILLER ... Campbell slit boy's throat

By STEPHEN MARTIN

MURDERER Jason Campbell will NOT be transferred to Belfast's Maze prison.

He will serve his life sentence in Scotland, Government sources revealed last night.

There had been furious protests over plans to treat Campbell as a political prisoner.

Now Scots Secretary Donald Dewar has ordered an urgent review of the decision.

A Scottish Office spokesman said: "Donald Dewar is reconsidering the case."

He refused to elaborate on when the review would be completed or why it had been launched.

But a top-level Downing Street source confirmed it would mean the killer serving his sentence here.

The dramatic U-turn

TURN TO PAGE NINE

149

Daily Record

Saturday, October 11, 1997 — 30p

SCOTLAND'S CHAMPION

FLY TO LONDON

EXCLUDES £10 AIRPORT TAX

Call us direct in the UK

FOR £12

YOU CAN'T BEAT THE RECORD FOR FARE DEALS

PAGES 20 & 21

LIED ... Campbell

Killer's fake uncle

EXCLUSIVE
By ANNA SMITH

KILLER Jason Campbell lied about a fake uncle to con his way into Belfast's Maze jail.

Last night, Scottish Secretary Donald Dewar confirmed the Record's exclusive report that Campbell would be staying in Scotland.

He said Campbell's application should not have been granted and the case had, "not been handled as it should

TURN TO PAGE NINE

BEER WE GO!

Pub army set for roaring success

SHOUTING THEM IN ... Scots stars Craig Burley and Colin Hendry

THE whole of Scotland is set for a wild World Cup party today.

Our Braveheart boys are just 90 minutes away from next year's finals in France.

Pubs will be packed as fans watch them lay into the Latvians live on TV.

Thousands more will roar on the team at home. And the Tartan Army are in no

By ALLISON McLAUGHLIN

doubt who's going to win – punters have staked £1million on a Scotland victory.

The football party could go on for hours – many supporters will carry on drinking as they cheer Italy's bid to oust England later tonight.

But the lucky ones are the 50,000 fans who'll be roaring the team to victory

TURN TO PAGE TWO

Daily Record

Tuesday, October 21, 1997   30p

SCOTLAND'S CHAMPION

Megan: Man is charged

A JOBLESS labourer was last night charged with the murders of Lin Russell and her daughter, Megan.

Michael Stone, 37, is also accused of attempting to murder 10-year-old Josie Russell.

She survived the cornfield attack which left her mum and sister dead from horrific head injuries.

Stone, of Gillingham, Kent, will appear before

PAGE TWO

Armed stalker is freed

STALKER victim Kate Hall is living in fear after a judge freed the knife thug who terrorized her.

David Williamson, 35, held her hostage in her Kirkcaldy home then wrote to her from his cell threatening to kill her with a shotgun.

And last night, Kate wept: "I believe he'll do it this time."

FULL STORY PAGE NINE

BARR 'SOLD MEAT AFTER E COLI SCARE'

IN COURT...E Coli charge butcher John Barr yesterday

BUTCHER John Barr was yesterday accused of selling meat AFTER a food poisoning scare at his shop.

It's claimed he supplied it for a party last November – the day after being alerted to an E Coli outbreak.

And when the anxious customer

Court charge

called to check if it was safe, Barr allegedly told him not to worry.

The 55-year-old butcher is on trial for wilfully and recklessly selling meat from his shop in Wishaw, Lanarkshire.

FULL STORY – PAGES 4 AND 5

Daily Record

Thursday, October 23, 1997   30p

SCOTLAND'S CHAMPION

THE FINAL 4 HOURS

I GAVE DIANA LAST RITES

PAGES 4&5

BLAIRY LEGS ... Tony

Tony is all set to Blair his legs

By KEVIN MAGUIRE

TONY Blair is to serve up a treat for the girls by baring his legs for the first time in public.

The Premier will put on shorts to play tennis at this weekend's Edinburgh Commonwealth summit.

Blair, 44, wants a game with one of the other leaders. His aides are scouring the guest list for someone young enough to play him on Sunday.

The PM won a leaders' bike race at the Euro summit in Amsterdam in June. And he's out for another victory.

A Downing Street spokesman joked: "Obviously, his tennis partner will have to be someone he can beat."

Blair and wife Cherie will take world leaders including South Africa's Nelson Mandela to St Andrews for tennis and golf.

The £7million conference, with its laser shows, fireworks, choirs and musicians, is intended to show off Britain as a "young country".

MORSE ROW – Page Nine

AGONY: *Lethal beam aimed at driver of fire engine*

LASER YOB BURNS 999 HERO'S EYE

By PETER LAING

A THUG armed with a laser burned a hole in a fireman's eye.

Mercy man Gordon Anderson, 38, was driving his fire engine back from a 999 call when the powerful light beam bored into his left eye.

It left him in agony and unable to see.

Gordon's furious colleagues reckon teenage yobs carried out the attack, using a tiny laser pen that can easily be bought in shops.

Fife firemaster Nigel Campion stormed: "Our guys put themselves in enough danger without Star Wars being declared on them."

He believes sales of the lasers should be tightly controlled.

Gordon needed hospital treatment after the assault in Glenrothes, Fife.

Station officer Iain Kelly said: "The

TURN TO PAGE FIVE

FLY TO LONDON FOR £12   **PAGE 41** Excludes £10 airport tax

Daily Record

Friday, October 24, 1997 — 30p

SCOTLAND'S CHAMPION

CAMERON'S IN LOVE
HAPPY DIAZ!
WOW EXCLUSIVE – PAGES 60 and 61

SWEETHEARTS ... Karen Martin and Toby Exley died in their car

Stockcar racer is charged on rage deaths

By ADRIAN SHAW

A STOCKCAR racer was charged with manslaughter last night over the road rage deaths of sweethearts Toby Exley and Karen Martin.

Jason Humble, 32, will appear before magistrates in London today.

He was arrested with motor dealer Keith Collier, 49, in a dawn raid on the home they share.

Chef Toby, 22, and girlfriend Karen, 20, died when their car was allegedly rammed across a barrier into oncoming traffic.

The deaths of the young couple on a west London dual carriageway shocked the nation and led to a massive police hunt for the driver of the car said to have shunted them.

Their heartbroken families begged the driver to give himself up.

The pair arrested yesterday were taken to a police station where they were quizzed throughout the day.

Collier will also appear at the court,

TURN TO PAGE SEVEN

DEALERS IN MISERY: *Evil gang sentenced to 53 years*

HEROIN MR BIG CAGED

SANTINI ... ran Scotland's most powerful heroin pushing racket

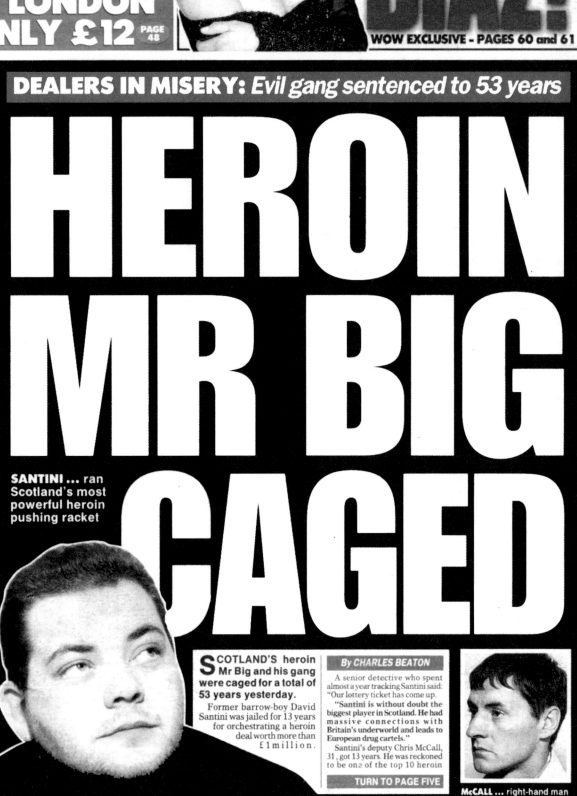

S COTLAND'S heroin Mr Big and his gang were caged for a total of 53 years yesterday.

Former barrow-boy David Santini was jailed for 13 years for orchestrating a heroin deal worth more than £1million.

By CHARLES BEATON

A senior detective who spent almost a year tracking Santini said: "Our lottery ticket has come up.

"Santini is without doubt the biggest player in Scotland. He had massive connections with Britain's underworld and leads to European drug cartels."

Santini's deputy Chris McCall, 31, got 13 years. He was reckoned to be one of the top 10 heroin

TURN TO PAGE FIVE

McCALL ... right-hand man

sunday mail

55p   October 26, 1997   4157

CLOCK THIS!

FREE WATCH

It's time to change...

Get a new watch FREE when you buy one from us **Page 23**

FREE XS

Twiggy gets catty over the catwalk queens

£12 FLIGHTS
0990 800 226

Bonus token and booking form **Page 6**

KISS OF DEATH!

Timebomb lover first in Britain to face Aids charges...

EXCLUSIVE

THIS young woman is a walking timebomb.

For Stella Nelson's former boyfriend claims that she infected him with the deadly AIDS virus.

And yesterday it was revealed that Stella, 32, has had a string of lovers.

They say she had unprotected sex with them. Now Wayne Simpson, 28, wants mum-of-four Stella CHARGED with giving him the virus when they were lovers.

Police are investigating the claims and Stella could make history as the first woman in Britain to face such charges.

Yet in an amazing twist Wayne last night claimed he still LOVES her.

FULL STORY–PAGE 5

The roof fell in on baby Fergus ... it should have killed him but he just kept on snoozing

FULL AMAZING STORY – Page 7

154

Daily Record

Monday, October 27, 1997 — 30p

SCOTLAND'S CHAMPION

ONE 2 ONE SPECIAL
A-Z OF BOND BABES
Centre Pages

PRESSURE ... Swire

Premier rejects Mandela plea on Lockerbie

By KENNY FARQUHARSON

TONY Blair yesterday rejected a plea from Nelson Mandela to let the Lockerbie bombing suspects face trial abroad.

The Prime Minister told the South African president the two Libyans had nothing to fear from a Scottish court.

But the Government was coming under intense pressure last night to back down.

Blair was yesterday warned by relatives of the Lockerbie victims that he risked "poisoning his reputation" by refusing to budge on a neutral venue for a trial.

Dr Jim Swire, who lost his daughter, Flora, in the 1988 Lockerbie bombing, which claimed 270 lives, said:

"We are talking human anguish and brutal premeditated murder of totally innocent lives.

"It is our tragedy, not the property of politicians and lawyers to play with as they like."

He added: "With President Mandela now beside us, we say to our new

TURN TO PAGE TWO

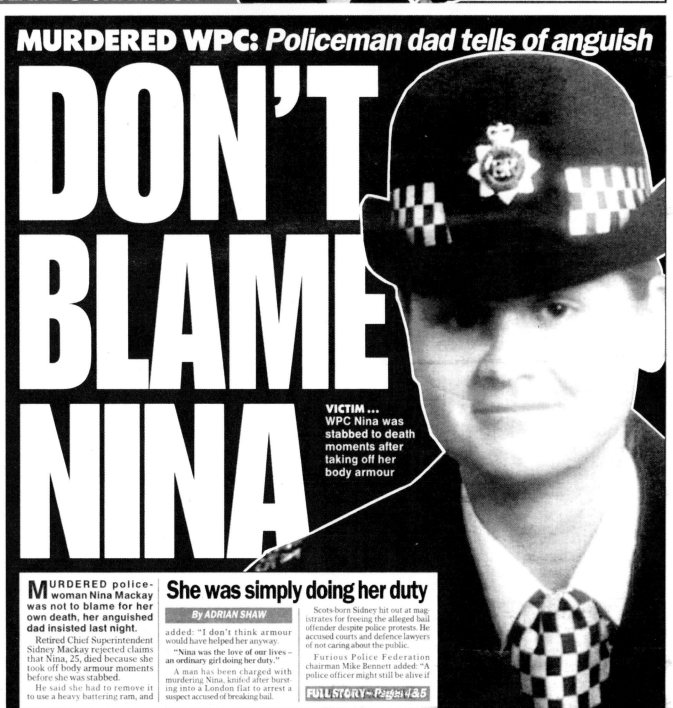

MURDERED WPC: *Policeman dad tells of anguish*

DON'T BLAME NINA

VICTIM ... WPC Nina was stabbed to death moments after taking off her body armour

---

MURDERED policewoman Nina Mackay was not to blame for her own death, her anguished dad insisted last night.

Retired Chief Superintendent Sidney Mackay rejected claims that Nina, 25, died because she took off body armour moments before she was stabbed.

He said she had to remove it to use a heavy battering ram, and

She was simply doing her duty

By ADRIAN SHAW

added: "I don't think armour would have helped her anyway.

"Nina was the love of our lives – an ordinary girl doing her duty."

A man has been charged with murdering Nina, knifed after bursting into a London flat to arrest a suspect accused of breaking bail.

Scots-born Sidney hit out at magistrates for freeing the alleged bail offender despite police protests. He accused courts and defence lawyers of not caring about the public.

Furious Police Federation chairman Mike Bennett added: "A police officer might still be alive if

FULL STORY ~ Pages 4 & 5

Daily Record

Tuesday, October 28, 1997   30p

...TLAND'S CHAMPION

NEW MAN AT IBROX?

BACK PAGE

EXCLUSIVE

911 STAR

I DIDN'T SCORE WITH GIGGS LOVER

PAGE 3

Death rap nanny's gamble

MURDER charge nanny Louise Woodward has taken a sensational gamble on her performance in the dock.

Louise, 19, has opted for an all-or-nothing verdict from the jury in Massachusetts.

It means she will spend at least 15 years in jail over the death of baby Matthew Eappen if convicted – or walk free.

Louise, from Cheshire, is hoping her show in the dock will sway the jury.

SEE PAGE TWELVE

Five-year lifeline for Pound

BRITISH shoppers could be using the new Euro currency as early as 2002.

Chancellor Gordon Brown told the Commons yesterday that if the single currency works, Britain should join it.

He said we would not be taking part as the first wave of countries takes up the single currency in 1999.

But if the British public backs it in a referendum, we could sign on for the Euro after the next General Election.

SEE PAGE TWO

FIASCO

Families' fury as E Coli case folds

CLEARED... John Barr at court yesterday

THE collapsed trial of butcher John Barr was branded a £100,000 fiasco last night.

Relieved Barr, 52, was sensationally cleared yesterday of recklessly supplying meat for an 18th birthday party after being ordered not to.

A sheriff threw out the Crown's case, ruling there wasn't enough evidence to back it up.

Angry MPs asked why the complex and costly case was

By ROGER HANNAH and IAIN FERGUSON

brought, only to fail so spectacularly.

And there were renewed calls for a full public inquiry into the outbreak of E Coli food poisoning, centred on Barr's home town of Wishaw, Lanarkshire, which claimed 20 lives.

Barr was accused of sending suspect beef, ham and turkey to a party for teenager Lauren MacFarlane at a pub in Wishaw.

The MacFarlanes were stunned at the sudden collapse of the case. Lauren's angry dad William said: "I don't

understand why the Crown went ahead if there was a lack of evidence.

"My family has been under considerable stress for the past 11 months. The case should have been better prepared."

Lib-Dem legal affairs spokesman Menzies Campbell was horrified at the court shambles.

He said: "A great deal of public money has been spent to no effect. The Lord Advocate should consider very carefully why this case was ever brought."

Barr refused to comment on his acquittal.

He faces returning to court in January, to face charges of breaking food hygiene rules at his Wishaw shop.

TREATED LIKE CRIMINALS ~ Pages Four & Five

Daily Record

Wednesday, October 29, 1997 30p

SCOTLAND'S CHAMPION

HOW TO SLEEP EAZZZY
inside *THE MAX!*

TRAGEDY: *Police haul missing car from river*

BABY BLUES MUM AND GIRL, 7 DEAD

By SHAUN MILNE and CHARLES BEATON

THE bodies of a missing mum and daughter were found in a car at the bottom of the Clyde yesterday.

Morag Nicolson, who had post-natal depression, disappeared 10 days ago with seven-year-old Samantha.

She told her hubby "I love you" and drove off to buy newspapers. But she and Samantha were never seen again.

LOST ... Morag and Sam

FULL STORY ~ Pages 4 & 5

Murray's tribute to Walter

●RANGERS chairman David Murray last night admitted he'll NEVER be able to replace Walter Smith.

The Ibrox manager yesterday confirmed his decision to quit at the end of this season.

Murray said: "Walter is the last of a breed.

"I don't think we'll have another manager with his integrity and loyalty."

BACK PAGE

Sex fiend Cronin is caged

● SERIAL sex fiend John Cronin yesterday admitted using false names to dupe women into spending time with him.

One of the aliases he used was of a member of the family that runs Jenners department store in Edinburgh.

After a bizarre legal wrangle at Edinburgh Sheriff Court, the 26-year-old was remanded in custody.

PAGE NINE

PLAY £25,000 SCRATCH *PAGE 20* **WIN A VIP FOOTBALL TRIP** *PAGE 41*

Daily Record

Thursday, October 30, 1997   30p

SCOTLAND'S CHAMPION

TOP OF THE POPPIES

GIRLS LAUNCH APPEAL—Page 7

Thugs glue girl, 13 to kids' playride

By STEPHEN RAFFERTY

SICK thugs trapped a teenage girl by supergluing a play-park roundabout.

The 13-year-old jumped on the ride using both hands and became stuck fast.

A group of boys were hanging around the play area at the time of the incident.

Fire crews used cutting gear to free the youngster. She was taken to hospital with 18inches of the metal post attached to her hands.

The teenager's ordeal started last night when she was playing with friends at a swingpark in Rowan Drive, Blackburn, West Lothian.

Ambulance controller Jimmy Thomson said: "Someone left superglue or Bostik on the barrier.

"This appears to be an act of badness on someone's part."

A Lothian and Borders Fire Brigade spokeswoman said: "The girl went to St John's Hospital in Livingston."

The unnamed girl was released after treatment in casualty.

WRECKER: *Jackson dashes hopes of bringing home Sapphire dead*

GLENDA'S CRUEL SEA SNUB

THE grieving families of four lost fishermen were cruelly snubbed by Glenda Jackson yesterday.

The shipping minister spurned their plea to raise the wreck of Peterhead trawler the Sapphire and give the bodies of the crew a decent burial.

Jackson even told them: "The sea is a noble resting place."

FULL STORY ~ Pages 4 and 5

NO... Jackson

FREE CAN OF MILLER LAGER

FOR OVER 18s ONLY... AVAILABLE AT SELECTED EDINBURGH OUTLETS

PAGE 37

Daily Record

Friday, October 31, 1997   30p

SCOTLAND'S CHAMPION

GUILTY

Dad's grief as wife and three kids die in blaze

By SHAUN MILNE and GRACE McLEAN

YOUNG dad David Wilson was in torment last night after his wife and three young children were killed in a fire at their home.

David, 23, battled in vain to save Michelle, 22, daughters Jackie, three and Katie, two, and eight-month-old son Brian.

He sobbed : "I have nothing left. My life is shattered. What am I going to do without them?"

As he recovered in hospital, David

TURN TO PAGE FIVE

PERISHED ... Katie, Jackie, Brian and, inset, Michelle with David

Nanny gets life for the murder of baby Matt

3AM NEWS By ANDY LINES

NANNY Louise Woodward was this morning sensationally found guilty of murdering baby Matthew Eappen.

After the verdict was read out, the 19-year-old collapsed and wept uncontrollably.

She sobbed: "I didn't do it. I didn't do anything."

The conviction on the charge of second-degree murder means Louise now faces an automatic life sentence.

She will not be eligible for parole for at least 15 years.

There was uproar in the court as the verdict was

SHATTERED ... Louise

announced. Louise's lawyers tried to comfort her as she shouted: "Why did they do this to me?"

Her parents, Gary and Sue looked on in disbelief.

After calm was restored, judge Hiller Zobel ordered

TURN TO PAGE 13

SPICE CARDS

FREE
SEE PAGE 34

Daily Record

Saturday, November 1, 1997　　30p

SCOTLAND'S CHAMPION

Why did they do this to me .. I'm only 19

Judge is last hope as Louise gets life

STUNNED Louise Woodward screamed "Why? I didn't do anything" as she was sent down for life yesterday.

The 19-year-old au pair collapsed in tears after being found guilty of murdering baby Matthew Eappen.

She sat sobbing in the dock and

From ANDY LINES IN Boston

said: "Why did they do that to me – I'm only 19."

But in a dramatic twist last night, it emerged that Louise may still go free.

Maverick trial judge Hiller Zobel

will decide on Tuesday whether to let the murder charge stick – or throw it out. The defence team will plead for the verdict to be over-turned or for a retrial.

And Zobel astonished legal experts by offering Louise a third way out. He said he would consider
TURN TO PAGE TWO

PARENTS TWIST KNIFE: Pages 2 & 3 ● **SHE'D NEVER KILL:** Pages 4 & 5 ● **SELFISH AND STUPID:** Pages 8 & 9

WOMEN SPECIAL

ARE YOU A DEVIL IN BED?

PAGES 20&21

OWNED UP ... Helen Percy

I confess says sex row Rev Helen

EXCLUSIVE
By ANNA SMITH

A CHURCH minister yesterday confessed to having sex with a married elder of the Kirk.

The Rev Helen Percy had told a Church of Scotland inquiry that she never slept with him.

But last night, Helen owned up in an exclusive interview with the Record.

The 32-year-old minister told how farmer Sandy Nicoll climbed into her sick bed as she lay suffering from flu.

Froze

Close to tears, she said: "Sandy came to my farmhouse with some hot soup. He ended up in my bed.

"I loved him as a father figure. But when he climbed into my bed I just froze."

The sex shame has rocked the Church of Scotland and stunned people in Helen's rural parish.

Sandy Nicoll and his wife Moyra have split up and their farm has been sold.

And tonight, Kirk officials will decide whether to take Helen to the Church of Scotland's own

TURN TO PAGE FIVE

Families launch cash appeal

HELP US RAISE THE SAPPHIRE

PLEA FOR HELP ... Families of the Sapphire victims

RELATIVES of the four fishermen lost aboard the Sapphire will today ask the public to help bring their loved ones home.

They will launch a public appeal for £380,000 to raise the sunken trawler from the bottom of the North Sea.

The families, left in the lurch

EXCLUSIVE By
BOB DOW and CHARLIE GALL

when the Government refused to help them, must get all the money by the weekend if their men are to be brought home for burial.

With bad weather on the way, the barge needed for the salvage is only available for a few more days.

The Daily Record and its sister paper, the Sunday Mail, immediately promised £10,000 for the campaign.

FULL STORY ~ Page 6-7

Daily Record

Tuesday, November 11, 1997   30p

SCOTLAND'S CHAMPION

LOUISE FREED!

ROAD TO FREEDOM ... Louise Woodward is driven from court yesterday

MERCY ... Judge Zobel

LOUISE Woodward was sensationally freed last night.

Judge Hiller Zobel reduced the 19-year-old au pair's murder conviction to manslaughter, then said the 279 days she spent in jail after her arrest was punishment enough.

Louise, 19, thought she was facing 10 years jail. She vowed to fight on to prove her innocence of killing baby Mattie Eappen.

But her dreams of coming

By ANDY LINES

home to Elton, Cheshire, were dashed when prosecutors launched a legal bid to put her back in jail.

Zobel said: "It is time to bring this extraordinary matter to a compassionate conclusion."

Louise left the court in Cambridge, Massachusetts, with her overjoyed parents Gary and Sue.

FULL STORY ~ *Pages 2 and 3*

Blunders that led to Scott's murder

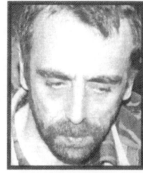

FREE TO KILL ... pervert Leisk

By STEVE SMITH, BOB DOW and CHARLIE GALL

TWO shocking blunders left sex monster Steven Leisk free to kill little Scott Simpson.

The paedophile, caged for life yesterday, was meant to be under supervision when he strangled nine-year-old Scott.

But Leisk's social worker hadn't seen him for **EIGHT WEEKS** before the murder. And his dithering bosses didn't bother to tell police Leisk was living yards from a playground. The

TURN TO PAGE FOUR

INNOCENT VICTIM ... Scott